LEAVING THE ENCHANTED FOREST

LEAVING THE ENCHANTED FOREST

The Path from Relationship Addiction to Intimacy

Stephanie Covington

and

Liana Beckett

1817

Harper & Row, Publishers, San Francisco

New York, Grand Rapids, Philadelphia, St. Louis
London, Singapore, Sydney, Tokyo, Toronto

Library of Congress Cataloging-in-Publication Data
Covington, Stephanie.
    Leaving the enchanted forest.

    Bibliography: p.
    1. Love.   2. Compulsive behavior.   3. Intimacy
(Psychology).   4. Women—Socialization.   5. Co-dependence
(Psychology).   I. Beckett, Liana.   II. Title.   III. Title:
Relationship addiction to intimacy.
HQ801.C734   1988   306.7   88-45130
ISBN 0-06-250163-1 (pbk.)

    90 91 92 HC 10 9 8 7

We dedicate this book to our readers. May it
become a pathfinder's companion on the journey
to the personal rediscovery of an intimate,
separate self in wholesome relationship.

Contents

Acknowledgments

Success requires more than teamwork—it requires a great team. In successfully carrying this project to completion, from the unfolding seed of an idea to a finished book on a shelf, we have been fortunate in being guided, assisted, and supported by a great team.

Our special thanks go to our editorial consultant, Roy M. Carlisle of Mills House, whose vision, encouragement, and expertise sustained us and guided us throughout. We are grateful to our editor Tom Grady at Harper & Row, whose insights and support made the editorial process stimulating and smooth, and to Linda Chester, literary agent extraordinaire. We also want to thank friends and colleagues who supplied us with valuable feedback and comments at various stages of completion.

This book is about relationships—about the things we have learned not only in our professional associations but especially in our own relationships throughout the years. The people who have populated our lives are the core of the team. They were our teachers; without them, this book would not have been possible. And so we wish to express our gratitude to the clients who provided us with useful insights for the vignettes interspersed in the narrative and the ones whose teaching are written between the lines. And we thank and celebrate our families, our sons and daughters—Judy and Gerry B.; Kim and Richard C.—former husbands, former and present lovers, friends, psychotherapists, and gurus. Because their lives and ours at some point touched in powerful ways, each one of them lives in these pages and in our hearts.

Finally, we want to thank one another and honor our friendship. It has survived the winds of change and the inevitable tests and challenges of making personal statements with a common voice. We learned much from each other; ultimately, our mutual caring and personal goodwill became the glue that lends meaning to the strings of words.

Introduction

Much new ground has been broken in the addiction field in the past decade. Starting from a core of work on alcoholism and drug addictions, the echoes of this pursuit have spread to other, more diffuse addictions. In the past four years the public has come to realize that whether the "addictive substance" is alcohol, food, work, money, or another person, the underlying addictive process is essentially the same.

Women, especially, have identified with relationship addiction. Many were jolted into realizing that the problems associated with their unhealthy dependence on their partners was anything but unique, and that their unhappy relationships had identifiable causes and predictable courses and consequences. But once convinced, these same women found themselves at a loss for healthier alternatives, for better frames of reference, for new models, for finer discriminations—for healing themselves and the generational cycle of family addictions and dysfunctional relationships.

What is an optimally functioning family? What are the signs of a healthy relationship? What are its elements? Will I know a positive one when I see one? What do I look for in selecting a partner? Will I know a desirable one when I see one? What do I need—and how do I need to change—to be in a relationship that is both healthy and satisfying? These are legitimate questions, and they are universal.

The complexity of our lives and times places tremendous stress on relationships. Today, people change jobs, home, and community more often than in the past. The more frequent willingness of professional women to relocate in pursuit of promotions and career paths adds a new dimension of intricacy to their relationships. And, living as we do in the United States of the late 1980s, we also live in an age of compulsivity, a frenetic activity-oriented climate that encourages and venerates excess, volume, and hyperbole. "Conspicuous consumption" may be an outdated term, but its reality is very much with us. Endlessly in pursuit of new highs, we drink, eat, smoke, pop pills, spend, and travel more per capita than anyone else on the planet. The *legal* mood-altering drug industry alone grossed $13.5 billion in 1985. And research shows that, despite the liberated 1970s, more people are having more sexual problems—the increase is particularly notable in difficulties of inhibited sexual desire. Small wonder. We attempt to numb the gaping void inside with the quick fix of sex, drugs, and excitement, when what we really long for is intimate contact with others and with our higher selves. Today, you don't have to qualify as a relationship addict to find it difficult to maintain a good relationship. And you don't need to have grown up in a dysfunctional family to wonder what makes for a healthy relationship or what makes the hard work of building a satisfying one worthwhile. The new focus on relationship addictions has sparked an intense scrutiny of all relationships and a public appetite for safe forums in which to discuss and work through issues of dependence and of unhealthy relating with the support of others with similar needs and goals. More people are going into psychotherapy with the stated goal to improve their relationships. Even people who come to therapy for other reasons spend much of the session working on relationship issues.

Unhealthy relating is commonly rooted in one's family of origin. Dysfunctional family systems come disguised in many packages; alcohol is merely one of many possible sources of dysfunction. One parent may have been emotionally unavailable because of extended physical or mental illness; another may have created an unstable, unpredictable environment because of emotional immaturity; yet another may have been victimized by economic and sociocultural deprivation and discrimination, with the family experiencing the severely stressful impact of psychological and physical deprivation of a society of plenty. Naturally, depending on these and many other factors, the degree of dysfunction also varies within each family. It must also be remembered that the concept of "dysfunction" is relative—it reflects the times and the social context. For example, relationships that would have seemed perfectly acceptable, perhaps even desirable, in the 1950s, may be considered dysfunctional or unhealthy today.

All in all, there seems to be a void of information, of guidelines and models, not only for the people who tend to become addicted to others or whose partners are themselves addicts of one kind or another, but for all those who are struggling to have better relationships in a world characterized by turmoil and unpredictability.

Leaving the Enchanted Forest is our attempt to narrow this gap. Models for new, healthier relationships are, in fact, around—not as many as we'd like yet, because the perspective is new and change is often difficult and slow. Also, because we live in an emotionally closed society and people want to protect their privacy, we are often unaware of the intricacies and challenges couples close to us are facing. We have known several of the couples we introduce in these pages personally and professionally; they have carefully and lovingly built lasting relationships that work for them and that support both partners' growth. Their relationships are models—*not* in the sense of "blueprints" that can be duplicated like cookbook recipes, but rather of guides for a process that leads to individual solutions that work well for that particular couple.

In writing this book, our primary aim has been to address the need of readers—especially women—to go one step beyond the awareness of being in unhealthy relationships in which they give away their personal power and sense of self. Many of you now are eager to develop new relationship skills and to channel creatively your newly discovered desire for self-empowerment and self-renewal. *Leaving the Enchanted Forest* addresses these needs by giving you the opportunity to review past and present relationships, thoughtfully reevaluate your personal beliefs and assumptions, and clarify who you are, what you need, what you want. For those who like structured activities to help them organize their thoughts, most chapters include exercises, writing activities, and experiential practices. These end-of-chapter activities can be used individually or by facilitators of groups for relationship addicts in recovery.

The book also includes information we hope will round out what you already know about addictions and family systems—including distinguishing characteristics of *optimal* families. However, we wish to appeal to those of you who may not relate to an alcoholic or otherwise dysfunctional family of origin. Don't put this book down because the terms don't seem to fit. Much of the time we do refer to the chemical dependency model to make a point. It is an excellent analogy for relationship addictions, one that will resonate with many readers—especially chemically dependent women in recovery for whom relationship addiction becomes a substitute for alcohol addiction. It is also a model we are familiar with in our work and through our belief in the power of twelve-step groups to heal both the addiction and the spirit. However, we also believe the information, activities, and inner work that *Leaving the Enchanted Forest* stimulates stand on their own. In contrast to other, similar books, many of the vignettes we have selected illustrate subtler, often neglected manifestations of dysfunction. We believe our approach will be of value to anyone who wants to gain a fresh perspective on what it means to love oneself while loving another—and is willing to work to develop the skills that can make it happen. At stake is nothing less than your ability to invest a more insightful, healthy, powerful, and freely choosing self in your present and future relationships.

Throughout, we have added a sociocultural dimension—looking beyond the family to factors inherent in the socialization of women that predispose them to dependent relationships. We have also chosen to move beyond the traditional relationship model of courtship and marriage. Over the past fifteen or twenty years, the structure of relationships has undergone major changes for large segments of our population. Some of our old traditions have been questioned; many of our psychotherapy clients struggle to find relationship options that suit them best, though they may be untraditional. Therefore, in order to reflect today's extraordinary diversity of people's lives, the vignettes and examples in this book describe a variety of relationship styles—including same-sex relationships. Because women identify much more readily with relationship addictions than men, the examples in the book are about women, and we have used the female pronoun throughout. However, this is not to deny that many men, past and present, are attached to women in addictive ways. The literature and opera librettos include many such male relationship addicts—Porgy in *Porgy and Bess,* and Don Giosé in *Carmen,* for example. (A notable difference is that, when the man is the addict, the woman he is addicted to is usually portrayed as an evil temptress.)

Finally, a word about the strong feelings that reading this book may awaken for some. Whenever we delve into our past to better understand the present, we accept a certain risk of reexperiencing past hurts, anger, and sadness. We accept the challenge because we have learned that ignoring and suppressing our feelings and our truths may spare us hurt for a while, but will not keep from harming us in the long run. We learn that to leave the past behind, we must first dare to face it.

Nonetheless, some childhoods are much more painful to confront than others. If you find that reading this book arouses disturbing emotions or troubling memories, don't try to handle them alone. Talk to a professional—preferably a psychotherapist or a minister. You may also find that reading part I of this book, which deals with your past, stirs a need in you to talk about newly discovered truths with your parents. Again, discuss your feelings and plans with a professional guide first.

Above all, we hope that after you put down this book you'll take with you an awareness that the learning and healing you are after comes from you—from you own hard work in unflinchingly looking at and telling your own truth.

Prologue: *Once Upon a Time . . .*

Since the days of courtly troubadours, the spell of romance has held us captive in the name of love. It has fanned our fantasies and daydreams, anesthetized our existential fears, and filled—albeit fleetingly—our inner voids. A sinecure in our searches for meaning and lasting love, romance has served as a catalyst for our dependencies and addictions to others. Romantic love and addictive, dependent love are two sides of the same dream.

In *We*, Robert Johnson, the well-known Jungian analyst and author, brings to life the destructive power of the romantic tradition by retelling the ill-fated romance of Queen Iseult the Fair and the knight Tristan.[1]

Having pledged allegiance to King Mark of Cornwall, young Tristan travels to Ireland to bring back Iseult the Fair, who is to become the king's bride. During their return voyage across the sea, Tristan and Iseult accidentally drink of a magic love potion. Hours later the two are found "still seated there, staring into each other's eyes, entranced and spellbound."

"For two days the love potion flowed in Tristan's veins and he suffered the agonies of love, now as though pierced by sharp thorns, now as though surrounded with sweet, fragrant flowers, and always the image of Iseult floated before his eyes." Thus Tristan and Iseult began a passionate love affair, breaching their promises, throwing caution to the winds. Although Iseult did become queen, the two lovers would not give each other up, continuing to see each other secretly, living a lie. Eventually they were caught and escaped together, taking refuge for more than three years in the enchanted forest of Morois. There "they lived on roots and herbs and the flesh of wild animals. Their skin stretched tight over their thin bodies, they were pallid and their clothes were ragged. But they gazed at one another, and the potion coursed in their blood, and they did not know that they suffered." A holy hermit challenged them to return to lawful living, but both Tristan and Iseult disclaimed the power to choose and to change—blaming the potion for their actions.

The powers of love potions are always ephemeral. Tristan and Iseult's lasted only to the end of the third year—three being a symbol of incompleteness and imbalance, and four a symbol of wholeness and completion. So it was in the fourth year that the

star-crossed lovers came back to their senses to see the hopeless-
ness of their situation and to hear the call of reality. Responding
to King Mark's overtures of forgiveness and reconciliation, the lovers finally left the enchanted forest. Queen Iseult the Fair returned
to her rightful place at the side of her husband. And Tristan left
Cornwall—but not before making a secret pact with Iseult that he
would always be true to her, accepting "her ring of green jasper as
token of her pledge to run to him any time he calls."

"Apart the lovers could neither live nor die, for it was life and
death together; and Tristan fled his sorrow through seas and is-
lands and many lands." His grief was unrequited. He longed for
death; finding no peace or pleasure in life away from his beloved,
Tristan lamented, "Will I never find someone to heal me of my
unhappiness?" After many years of wandering, fate answered Tristan's pleas, bringing into his life a lovely, gentle, and kind young
princess, Iseult of the White Hands. Despite her inner beauty and
devotion, Tristan could not love her, for he remained under the
spell of his romantic attachment to Iseult the Fair. Eventually, mor-
tally wounded by a poisoned spear, Tristan died, broken in body
and spirit, Queen Iseult's name on his lips.

The tragic irony of Tristan's story lies in his willful decision to
suffer and die for an idealized, illusive notion of love, blind to the
love that was available to him just for the asking. His receptivity
blocked by his own suffering and by his unrealistic image of Iseult
the Fair, Tristan's heart was closed to the effortless, rich promise
of a caring, gentle, committed earthly love relationship with Iseult
of the White Hands.

Tristan and Iseult the Fair sealed their own fate at the end of
their three-year escape into the enchanted forest of Morois. When
the fumes of the love potion started to clear, the lovers were at a
crossroads. The direction they chose would profoundly affect their
lives. Here was their chance to break the spell of their projections
and their fantasies. Now they could forge separate new paths that
would lead them out of the forest once and for all, helping them
rise to new levels of right relationship with themselves, with one
another, and with their community. Their resolve, however, was
too weak to accept complete surrender to an unknown and separate future. Missing the rich possibilities of the moment, they renewed their secret pact and their bondage with the exchange of
the jasper ring. "Refusing to graduate from Morois, they instead
find some winding path that will lead them back into the forest
meadows of their own projections."

According to Johnson, "It is every [individual's] fate to reach a
point in his life at which the spell is broken and he is called out of
the Forest of Morois." Like Tristan, many of us have experienced

the compelling attraction of the enchanted forest of our fantasies and addictions—at times lured by its wild, exotic, mysterious shadow play, at times skirting its edge, ready and willing to strike out and leave it behind forever, only to run back to it, fearful of the silence of the unknown beyond its familiar terrain. This book is dedicated to those who have heard the call, who keep testing the boundaries of the forest's enchantment within themselves.

Part I

THE PATH INTO THE FOREST

CHAPTER 1

The Love Potion: Chemistry and Dependence

On a recent TV talk show, the hostess asked about relationship addiction. She had heard the term a lot lately, she said, but was still puzzled. She asked, "Just what is relationship addiction? What does it really look like? Is it like any other addiction?" Her guest replied, "Well, it can show up in any number of ways: as an obsession, for example—a constant thinking, ruminating about the person you're in relationship with. Or there may be a compulsive quality about the behavior—for instance, making frequent detours just to drive or walk by the partner's work-place. There may also be signs of tolerance increase. In the relationship addict's case, this translates into needing more and more of the other person's presence to feel OK.

"There is a need to protect the supply, which shows up as an unrea-sonable degree of possessiveness or jealousy. And there may be symp-toms of withdrawal. When the relationship addict is separated from the 'source,' he or she may become anxious and depressed." "Hmm. . .," mused the show's hostess with a frown. "Sounds to me like you're de-scribing love!"

Although we have been socialized to think of this obsession as love, in fact, the compelling allure of its spell has little to do with the depth and enduring quality of true caring. Addiction to another person is what "falling in love" feels like—it is the wild abandon of the enchanted for-est. The crucial distinction between relationship addicts and other peo-ple who fall in love is that the former expect this fleeting phase of a relationship to become a utopian endless summer that sustains forever the poetry, the ecstasy, and the feelings of merger they experience in their infatuation. Not only have women been socialized to nurture and take care of men in relationship, but they—in particular—have believed the myth of romance.

As women, we have accepted the notion that if only we find the right person, we'll fall in love and live happily every after—as fairy tales promise. Given this stage setting, it is not surprising that even women who are not relationship addicts show many signs of dependence. But obsessions, compulsions, and the temporary high of being "in love" are neither love nor proof of love; on the contrary, they are the signposts of falling in love—that tempting ecstatic feeling that can so easily lead to dependence and addiction.

MARIA

At thirty-three, Maria has been a relationship addict most of her adult life. When she met Vic, Maria thought she had met her soulmate, a real-life version of the fairy tale prince: tall, dark, handsome, socially prominent, charming, and somewhat mysterious. Maria instantly fell for him. Within a few months they were married; like Tristan and Iseult, however, they did not live happily ever after.

When she fell in love with Vic, Maria misread some very important clues about him. She saw a superior man who was exciting, outgoing, friendly, and entertaining, but she saw him only in desirable contrast to her own alcoholic father—not in relation to herself. Unable to see past the glamour, she ignored warning signs about the inner man and failed to consider her inner needs or to ask herself what their life together might be like. As time went on, it became apparent that Vic was responsive to people only when he could be the center of attention. Because he was so self-centered, his delight in Maria's admiration was short-lived; he needed a challenge, a bigger audience. They became polarized: she became more focused on him, on trying to recapture his attention. But the harder she tried to get close to him, the more distant he became, escalating his involvement in his public and business life.

Maria became an extension of Vic, giving up her own aspirations and outside interests in favor of his. Soon her life became very narrow and isolated, and she was in constant emotional pain. Loneliness and abandonment, the things she feared most and had desperately tried to escape through relationships, kept creeping back into her life. To make matters worse, many of her friends had distanced themselves from her. They had become impatient with Maria, because despite her frequent tears, tales of woe, and pleas for sympathy, she often continued to stay in relationships that were clearly damaging to her health and self-esteem. Maria simply couldn't see it. She got her sense of self-worth from the rush of being in love and the initial admiration of the men she dated. With intense desperation she stubbornly continued to cling to her romantic dreams long after her men had turned their backs on her. So it was with her marriage to Vic. Even when she finally admitted to herself that it was not working, she could muster neither the courage nor the self-confidence to make the break until she had a new love in her life. The thought of having to face alone the emotional pain of a breakup terrified her. Not too surprisingly, this new relationship failed too, even though (or, rather, *because*) she focused all her energy and attention on the new man. Her fantasy that the right partner would fulfill all her needs—romantic love, excitement, self-worth, and the warding off of loneliness—continued into several other relationships.

THE SUBTLE NATURE OF RELATIONSHIP ADDICTION

Overall, relationship addiction follows a process common to all addictions. But although it does not differ in kind from other addictions, relationship addiction expresses itself in subtler ways than some other forms of addictive behavior. For one thing, many of the indicators of relationship addiction in women were considered acceptable, and even applauded, in the past. For example, when Maria married Vic, few of their friends thought it inappropriate or unwise for her to quit the job she loved or for her to give up her workout schedule so she could have more flexibility to adjust her schedule to his.

Another reason for the subtlety of relationship addiction is the fact that a fine line exists between desirable and undesirable degrees of behavior. Caretaking and other nurturing forms of behavior, for example, are aspects of any healthy relationship. Yet they may also be signs of an addictive relationship. The basic distinction is that in addiction the focus is on the significant other, to the detriment of yourself, not because you freely *choose* this, but because you are unable to say no to that person, being inordinately dependent and fearful of rejection and abandonment. One generic definition of addiction is "the chronic neglect of yourself in favor of someone or something else." The inability to control and change your behavior is a factor in all addictions, but in relationship addiction the operative words are *denial, anxiety,* and *fear*.

Finally, relationship addiction differs in a major way from addiction to alcohol and other drugs. A practicing alcoholic who wants to be sober needs to become abstinent and stop using the addictive substance totally. A relationship addiction, however, operates more like a food addiction; just as compulsive overeaters can't quit eating food entirely, so relationship addicts can't live in isolation and stop relating to others. Overeaters Anonymous cautions its members to abstain from "trigger foods." Likewise, if you fit the pattern of relationship addiction and are not in a current intimate relationship, you can learn to recognize and stay away from the type of person who tends to trigger your addictive behavior. Maria learned to recognize the type of man who might lead her into a slippery place—a situation in which she would place herself at high risk for relapse into her dependent behavior. For her, this was the "mysterious stranger," the dashing, exciting male who challenged her sense of intrigue by being aloof and withdrawn, barely acknowledging her presence.

On the other hand, you can be the architect of your own recovery even if you are in an addictive relationship. Experience shows that it often helps to take some time apart from your partner to break the cycle of addiction and to learn that you *can* survive on your own. Removing yourself, at least for a time, from the immediate influence of your trigger may be essential if you are to clarify your feelings, recharge your depleted energy, and learn to overcome your fear of abandonment. Learning from experience that you *can* leave the enchanted forest—and that you *can* get to the other side of your fear of abandonment and of the unknown—will help you start reclaiming your power.

HOW WE BECOME ADDICTED TO CERTAIN RELATIONSHIPS

Maria's single-minded focus on trigger men was only one indicator of relationship addiction—the most easily observable. But although her outer world kept falling apart, a powerful emotional process was also taking place. One way to understand what was happening in Maria's inner world is to follow the emotional evolution of her addiction through four stages typical of the addiction process.[1]

STAGE ONE: LEARNING THE MOOD SWING

At the beginning of each new relationship, Maria would experience the pleasant, intoxicating high typical of this early stage of involvement, the excitement of being attached to someone new. *The mood swing* (stage one) is caused by the adrenaline rush of romantic love and the pleasurable vicissitudes and tantalizing uncertainties typical of a new relationship. Focusing on her new partner also allowed her to avoid dealing with her own true emotional state. In this first stage all of Maria's emotional swings were positive, euphoric—all above the normal baseline, as shown in figure 1.

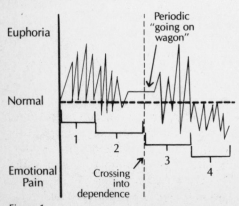

Four Stages of Relationship Addiction

1. Experiencing, and experimenting with, mood swing.
2. Seeking mood swing, going from euphoria back to normal. Physically negative experiences more frequent, but emotional price not significant yet.
3. Contact with partner for pleasure no longer primary. Maintaining contact mostly to relieve stress. Line to harmful dependence has been crossed.
4. Relating just to feel normal. Starting from position of emotional pain, likely to worsen with contact.

Figure 1
Source: Adapted from a model by Vernon Johnson in *I'll Quit Tomorrow* (San Francisco: Harper & Row, 1980).

STAGE TWO: SEEKING THE MOOD SWING

After a week or more of intense sexual and emotional connection with the new man, Maria would begin *seeking the mood swing* (stage two), looking forward to it, anticipating it. In this stage in the emotional development of her addiction, Maria's energy would be directed toward reexperiencing the high. She would become infatuated, starting to watch the clock, living in suspension until her lover's next phone call or their next date. She would readily give up many of her own activities and friendship commitments to spend more time with him, seeking greater involvement in his life as a solution to her own problems and as distraction from the issues in her own life. Such feelings and interpersonal dynamics are not unusual—they are the experience of falling in love.

At this stage some mood swing experiences would begin to be emotionally negative for Maria. At times the emotional pain of disagreements, distance or disconnection from her partner, or feelings of jealousy or rejection would offset the pleasure of his company. After such incidents Maria would be either embarrassed at having flown off the handle, dejected at having betrayed so much dependence, or panicked at the thought that her partner might leave. Overall, however, just as drinkers still believe that the fun had while intoxicated was well worth the suffering, Maria would keep wanting to believe, against growing evidence, that the man in her life was the wellspring of her joy and pleasure. Many of her mood swings would still be on the side of pleasure—but now several would also be *below* the normal baseline, the region of emotional pain. Her feelings of dejection or jealousy or panic would be more intense than her feelings of excitement or pleasure. But because at this point the emotional pain would still be bearable, Maria could manage the swing back to normal. She was not paying a significant emotional price yet. Periodically, Maria would "go on the wagon," which for her meant temporarily withdrawing from a relationship.

STAGE THREE: DEPENDENCE

At a certain point Maria would cross over the invisible line from infatuation into *dependence* (stage three). Her excessive focus on her lover shifted from being a choice to being a harmful neediness. Her life became narrow, unbalanced, unhealthy. As the relationship started to deteriorate, she would stay in it more out of her growing dependence than to recapture the lost sense of excitement and fun. She gave up so much of herself that she could conceive only of another man as the solution to her weakened sense of self and low self-esteem.

As the emotional investment and cost escalated, Maria would try to swing back from the depths of her pain and anxiety. But now she would often be unable to make it back to the normal baseline and her wrenching inner turmoil remained. Maria had lost control—yet even at this point she would be unaware that she was in trouble.

Typical indicators of Maria's harmful dependence were the obsessive thoughts constantly directed toward her lover and the compulsive behaviors. For example, Maria's inability to control her impulse to call her lover at all hours of the day or night and her need to drive by his office at odd times to check if his car was in the parking lot are typical addictive behaviors. As in a substance dependence, her "tolerance" would also increase—that is, she would need more contact with him in order to obtain the same momentary soothing effect that less frequent contact had previously provided. With her, this tolerance increase would often manifest itself in the frantic, insatiable quality of her sexual needs. *Decreased tolerance would then follow*—that is, Maria's personal boundaries would become so permeable that in any interaction with her lover, her loss of self would be almost immediate. During tolerance increase, Maria needed more and more of her partner; during tolerance decrease, she could hardly bear to be around him. Like all addicts, Maria would also anxiously "protect her supply," usually through emotionally exhausting, destructive scenes of jealousy and possessiveness. Finally, Maria at times would suffer withdrawal symptoms not unlike those of substance abusers: when a lover would cancel a date or show up late, she would frequently experience symptoms of anxiety and panic, such as sweating, dizziness, or trembling.

STAGE FOUR: MAINTAINING CONTACT TO FEEL NORMAL

From here, Maria would slip into an emotional state in which she had to *maintain close contact with her partner just to feel normal* (stage four); without him, she would be in a state of chronic emotional pain and depression. Exposure to the trigger person, originally aimed at making her feel euphoric, would no longer provide a true high. But even the slight lift it gave her was enough to maintain the self-destructive cycle. At this stage Maria experienced the equivalent of the alcoholic's blackout: a retreat into a fantasy world. But her very real feelings of free-floating anxiety, shame, and guilt would resurface, only making things worse. Her inner balance in shambles, she would unsuccessfully try to hide the chaos lurking just beneath the surface from family, friends, and employers, experiencing loss in every area of her life.

THE ADDICT'S INNER AND OUTER WORLDS

CONTRACTION

Another way to understand Maria's addiction is to look at both her inner—or intrapsychic—experience and at her outer world. Doing so

The Spiral of Addiction and Recovery

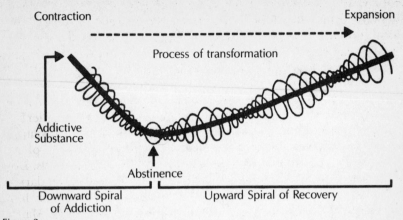

Figure 2

Source: Stephanie Brown, Ph.D., *Treating the Alcoholic: A Developmental Model of Recovery* (New York: John Wiley & Sons, 1985), p. 49.

helps to understand what happens to a relationship addict in ardent pursuit. From this perspective, Maria's process of addiction can be viewed as a progressive contraction of all aspects of her life—not only the physical and mental (her outer world), but also the emotional and spiritual (her inner world).[2]

Maria's relationship addiction can also be conceptualized as a downward spiral, where the focus of attention is on the trigger person, which is shown as a solid line at the center of the spiral in figure 2. For Maria, the solid line represents Vic and all the others who preceded and followed him.

The idea of *contraction* is perhaps the most useful single term to describe accurately what happened to Maria. Caught in an addiction, this bright and sensitive woman led a life that became increasingly narrow, unbalanced, impoverished, and diminished. Whenever she became involved in an addictive relationship, Maria would spend less and less time nurturing herself. In her marriage to Vic, in order to stay flexible for him, she gave up her evenings with friends, her physical fitness program, and even a psychologically and emotionally rewarding job. She hoped that Vic would ask her to join him on his frequent business trips. But that happened only twice, at the very beginning of their marriage.

By itself, contraction is not proof of addiction. But it is a valid indicator of an imbalance that often crosses over into addiction. Think of the recreational runners you know, for instance. Those least likely to become addicted to their sport are the ones whose lives have variety: they include time for work, for fun, for friends, for family—perhaps for community work and for hobbies. The people to be concerned about are those who become impatient at anything that interferes with their single-minded pursuit, cutting themselves off from any significant investment of time and care in relationships.

THE CONSEQUENCES OF ADDICTION

Substitution is one of the consequences of the addictive process. When people try to give up an addiction, they tend to substitute it with another. Besides being used to produce a high, the addictive substance is often used as a coping device that provides a soothing function for the user. Therefore it is common for people who are trying to give up their drug of choice to turn to another one. Cocaine users may tell themselves, "I won't use coke anymore. I'll just drink now and then." Alcoholics who stop drinking may start smoking pot or become workaholics, a substitution that is particularly insidious because hard work has always been sanctioned in our society.

Maria's substitution took the form of serial monogamy. Once she finally recognized that her relationship with Vic would not survive, she immediately sought out a replacement for him. Only then was she able to leave. Relationship addicts seem especially prone to substitute, not only by overlapping their relationships but also by overeating or running up large shopping spree bills. Both strategies are local anesthetics—ways to reduce their anxiety and fill the inner void. Shopping may also be an unconscious attempt to increase their sense of self-worth by buying "image" clothes—yet another way to seek a quick external fix.

Eventually any direct substitute for an addiction is bound to fail—whether it's organically grown marijuana, a more expensive brand of gin with fewer impurities, or yet another promising new partner. The illusions usually fail, but only when the addict has an experience that is personally intolerable. Maria eventually hit bottom when she was fired from a job she valued because of her unexplained absences, costly errors, and unacceptable mood swings. Having started yet another recent relationship that overlapped a very stressful previous one, she had been in a state of low energy and inner turmoil that affected her personal and professional life in negative ways. The self-destructive relationship cycle finally ended when Maria stopped lying to herself, surrendered, and was willing to start an inward journey of self-discovery and self-healing. Rather than continuing to focus, as she had in the past, on external situations and people to explain away her discomfort and pain, Maria began to examine her feelings, her thoughts, and the patterns in her life and her relationships. She found support for her new introspection in a Twelve-Step group (a self-help program based on the Twelve Steps or principles of recovery of Alcoholics Anonymous) she began attending regularly, in the insights she gained through psychotherapy, and in writing and sketching in her journal. She also gained increasing clarity and peace of mind from her spiritual practices.

RECOVERY AND EXPANSION

Just as she had experienced the spiraling contraction of addiction, now Maria experienced the upward process of recovery. The recovery spiral is anything but smooth. The path of recovery from addiction is filled with false starts, retraced steps, and pauses along the way. For all that, the overall pattern of the recovery spiral is characterized by *expansion*.

As shown in figure 2, even in recovery the object of your addiction— your trigger—remains the central focus: the solid black line that was at the center of the contracting addiction spiral is still there. This is an important reminder in anyone's recovery from addiction. Preserving a clear, unembellished memory of your addiction allows recovery to unfold; believing that you have fully recovered is a sure sign of trouble. You always need to remember what or who triggers your addiction, so you don't forget that you are vulnerable. To assume that your past addiction—or your addictability—has no lessons for your future is to risk repeating the past. There are no recovered addicts—only addicts who are recovering at different levels of the expansion spiral.

The upward spiral of recovery is not a mirror image of the downward process of addiction. The person in recovery has been changed—she will end up in a far different place from where she started. The Swiss analyst Carl Jung believed a spiritual transformation to be the only hope for alcoholics; in this experience of transformation lies the essential difference between the contraction of addiction and the expansion of recovery.

Although recovery can be an exciting adventure of finding yourself, of seeing yourself and the world with the freshness of a newborn, it can also be frightening, as all radical change can be. To some degree, most of us are frightened of the unfamiliar, the unknown. What is important is to accept that fear and uneasiness are something to be expected, a natural part of change. In time, when the unfamiliar becomes familiar, and with trust and faith, fear becomes manageable or disappears altogether. As Mark Twain said, "Courage is resistance to fear, mastery of fear, not absence of fear."

Maria began her recovery with a sense of trepidation. For the first time since her early teens, she was willing to face her fears of abandonment—knowing that they would lose their power only in facing them. She also allowed herself to risk being alone, which had been a frightening prospect all her life. And at first she was truly alone. Not only was she unemployed, but having made a break from her latest addictive partnership, her friendships and social life were also in shambles—they had died premature deaths from neglect. But gradually, as she focused

on her inner life to reconnect with her own sense of self, other friendships developed, and she was also able to breathe new life into some of
the old ones.

The paradox of recovery, Maria realized, was that in order for her
outer world to work, she had to focus on her inner world. As a relationship addict, she had always tried to be to her partners what she thought
they wanted her to be, losing sight of her own unique identity. Now she
had to draw on the inner source of her deepest knowing to find out
who the real Maria was. In her mind and her heart she moved backward
in time, reexamining her family of origin, recontacting and reparenting
her wounded inner child—the part of herself that still suffered from the
inadequate nurturing of her early years, the child she had disowned
until now. She developed a new understanding of love, intimacy, and
commitment, and the place of recovery and spirituality in her life and
relationships. Then, for the first time, she was able to identify her wants
in relationship as well as her bottom lines—the things she would no
longer be willing to do—or do without—in future partnerships.

STAGES OF RECOVERY

Early recovery is often a time in which certain kinds of substitution
can serve a useful function as a transition between addiction and ongoing recovery. Sometimes it is even encouraged by psychotherapists and
addiction counselors. It is important, however, for people in early recovery to select a substitute with positive outcomes. Chewing gum is more
positive than smoking pot. Working out at a gym is more positive than
overeating. Building self-esteem by becoming a skillful potter or pho-
tographer is more positive, and its long-range benefits are more lasting,
than buying a new silk dress. Being dependent for a time on the fellow-
ship of a support group or relationship-oriented Twelve-Step group
such as Al-Anon is more positive than being addicted to another person.

When Maria first began her recovery she started painting. Gradually
this pastime became more and more absorbing, until it had become a
major focus of her energy and weekly activities—at times at the expense
of a balanced life. This raises the question, Can a healthy substitute
become an addiction? There can be such a thing as a positive addiction,
provided two conditions are met. First, to be a positive addiction, it must
be one into which you put something of yourself. Working out, developing a skill, meditating, or painting, as Maria did, are examples of
potentially positive addictions. The addiction to alcohol or other drugs,
by this definition, is harmful and negative, because you add nothing of
yourself to get the exhilaration and soothing effect you seek.

Second, in contrast to a negative addiction, which creates contraction,
a positive addiction creates expansion in your life. Bob, for example, is
a man in his thirties who entered therapy to resolve a marital problem.
His therapist was well-trained in addictions. Right from the start, based

on his assessment of Bob's problems and his way of life, the therapist suspected chemical dependency but could find no indication of it. Yet, over and over, whenever he would try to make sense of Bob's experience, he would find himself thinking of Bob as alcoholic. He had all the characteristics of a negative addiction: chronic unemployment, isolation, lack of friends, disinterest in physical activity, unwillingness to participate in his wife's and children's activities in the evenings. After several months of therapy, one day the psychologist and Bob unraveled the puzzle: Bob was addicted to TV. The missing piece fell into place when Bob described a recent accident he had had on the freeway while watching a program on the new mini-TV he had bought for his car!

Even though Bob was neither an alcoholic nor a relationship addict, clearly he had a harmful, negative addiction: watching TV was a passive activity into which Bob put nothing of himself, and his life had all the signs of contraction and progressive dependence on the addictive substance. Because he couldn't afford a VCR, he missed work on the flimsiest pretexts to stay home and watch his favorite daytime programs. He had been placed on probation at work, and was in danger of losing his job because he had been unable to comply with the probation conditions. In the evenings and on weekends, he was emotionally distant and unavailable to his wife and children, which caused great imbalances and turmoil in his family.

In the wake of his automobile accident, Bob hit bottom. In the process of giving up his TV addiction, he experienced a tremendous void. Because the therapist knew Bob was likely to try to find a substitute in the process of recovery, the therapist guided him in exploring for himself some growth-enhancing options. Currently Bob is actively pursuing two newly discovered interests: he has taken up racewalking and has joined a scriptwriter's group. His new physical fitness program is putting him back in touch with himself. The writer's group helps him continue his interest in television in a more active way in a social setting.

MAKING CHOICES

At one time or another, many of us have walked the path into the enchanted forest of romance, dependence, and abandonment of the self. In the fog of denial, some become lost in the forest. Others, like Tristan and Iseult, venture to take a few steps away from the forest, only to allow fears and fantasies to block the way. Still others, having glimpsed the peaceful clearing beyond the wild brambles, step outside the forest, never to return, willingly accepting the insecurities of an unknown path, trusting that it will lead away from bondage and into personal freedom. You can create the path of your own recovery—the choice is yours.

CHAPTER 2

The Silver Cord: Family History

THE FAMILY AS SYSTEM

As much as we might like to believe that we are self-determined and self-directed, each of us is shaped by our past; who you are today is a mix of what you came into the world with and all your subsequent experiences. In that mix your family of origin has probably played one the most powerful roles, not only in who you are, but in how you live today. Families hand down across generations not only their genetic pool but also their blueprint for how to live in the world.

When this notion first sinks in, people often feel discouraged. It is hard to realize that your thoughts, emotions, and behavior are not as independently generated as you may have thought they were. And if your family of origin was dysfunctional, you might even start to feel hopeless, knowing that you are powerless to change the past.

In reality, a new understanding of the past can give rise to new hope. If you are willing to deepen your awareness of the role your family of origin is playing in your life today, you can begin the process of self-empowerment and self-change, leaving the past behind you and becoming the creator of your future path. Families are systems—units made up of a number of components that interact for common purposes or goals; the whole is greater than the total of its individual parts. A family system is like a mobile: each piece moves separately, yet all are interconnected. When one piece moves, every other piece moves to readjust until the mobile has found a new point of balance. In a family, when some major change takes place in the life of one of its members, every other member shifts. This is true for all change—not necessarily just for negative situations or crises. A son may get married, a daughter may go away to college, a mother may go into treatment for alcoholism, a father may dramatically change the amount of time spent at home because of a new job. In terms of how the various family members relate to one another, it is of secondary importance whether the father now spends a lot less or a lot more time at home: *the real issue is the sudden, dramatic change.* Change, in itself, will cause every family member to undergo the realignment that eventually will allow the family system to assimilate the new situation into a new balance.

SARAH'S FAMILY

Recently Sarah, an attractive, tanned woman in her thirties, walked into her therapist's office smiling, and flopped her tall, slightly stooped figure gracefully into a chair. She was feeling a little smug that day, she said. A few days earlier she had entertained her parents and brother. Unlike previous times, however, during this visit she had noticed the covert dance of subtle tensions, veiled messages, and predictable patterns of interaction in which everyone took part.

Sarah told her therapist that it had all started with an invitation to her family to join her husband, Scott, herself, and their children for a New Year's Day supper. She had spent several hours cooking and making sure everything was in its place. She recalled that while she placed the finishing touches onto the festive table setting she had been worried. Would her flamboyant mother find the floral centerpiece too small, too bland? Would her brother, Nate, think the table setting too formal? Too sweet for his taste? Sarah and her older brother had a great liking for each other, yet Sarah had always been a little intimidated by Nate's achievements, independence, and polish. "Thank heaven for Dad," she had sighed. At least he could always be relied on not to say much—one way or another.

Sarah said that at that point she had caught herself, noticing how negative and self-critical she was being. She had consciously set aside her self-doubts, allowing her senses to come alive as she surveyed the scene. She had looked toward the kitchen; a tantalizing aroma wafted her way from the casserole that was baking in the oven.

The buzz of Scott's saw in the garage was comforting. Praise the Lord and Scott's good nature, the hamster would finally have a home of its own by the next day; then she could lay claim to the laundry tub again. Things were really starting to fall into place.

On her way back to the kitchen, Sarah had stopped in front of the hall mirror for a last check, peering into her myopic gray eyes appraisingly. She had brushed her cheeks and the corners of her mouth lightly with her fingertips, glad not to find any new wrinkles. Raising her blouse collar at a pert angle, and fluffing her short blond curls, she had grinned at her image, "Not bad!" At that moment she had felt pleased with herself—and grateful for her life and her family.

Then the doorbell had rung, and everyone had rushed toward the front door, Scott still brushing sawdust from his bushy eyebrows and beard. Sarah had placed a quick peck on his cheek. Within seconds the hall had been filled with people all talking at once, hugging one another in a confusion of laughter, chatter, and warmth.

Sarah told the therapist that suddenly she had noticed that her mother, father, and brother were loaded down with platters, bowls, and dishes. Caught off-guard, she had turned to her mother and said, "I thought we agreed that I would take care of all the food today." Laura, her imposing, white-haired mother, had responded firmly, "Yes, I know, dear. But then I decided to cook a roast beef dinner anyway, just in case your dad doesn't like your fancy French cooking." Not waiting for a reply, she had brushed past Sarah into the kitchen and toward the refrigerator, husband and son in tow. Nate had winked at Sarah, scarcely able to contain his amusement. Sarah had responded in kind, rolling her eyes upward in mock martyrdom. She and her brother had always managed to survive the family's oddities and the hurts they dealt by filtering them through the wildly irreverent humor they shared only with one another.

Actually, it had been their mother who had acted most annoyed, Sarah recalled. Scrutinizing the contents of the refrigerator with a scowl, she had demanded, "How come there's no room in here? This food needs to be refrigerated!" Sarah, recognizing a familiar pattern, had refused to match her mother's mood. She had laughed, reminding her mother archly that because she hadn't looked into her crystal ball lately, she could scarcely have divined that she ought to be clearing space for a second full-course meal that day. Laura had laughed too. The tension had been broken.

Meanwhile Doug, Sarah's father, had set the platter he had been carrying on the counter. Sarah had watched him with concern as he had loosened his tie and opened the pantry to fix himself a drink. Without a word he had walked into the den to watch a pregame show on TV. Sarah said that it had been obvious he was irritated that Laura had made him the cause of the fuss. Her father never seemed to care one way or another what he ate. Even though he never rebelled openly, it was clear that he resented being dominated and used by Laura as a foil for her manipulations.

With a certain sense of detachment, Sarah told her therapist that she had found the whole situation rather amusing. "Typical of my family," she commented. "All this energy around food, and Mother always having to be in charge, always the center of activity and attention." She told the therapist that, based on previous family holidays, she could almost have predicted how the conversation would proceed at the dinner table that day, had she not intervened. She and Scott would bicker over whether the twins should be allowed to have dessert without finishing their dinner. Laura, oblivious to the extra twenty pounds she was carrying on her frame, would needle Scott about the amount of butter he spread on his biscuits and the paunch he had put on since marrying Sarah. He would just laugh it off good-naturedly and keep on doing exactly what he wanted to do. But Sarah would take on the guilt, and go on a crash diet the next day to lose her extra weight, continuing a constant cycle of dieting and overeating. Nate, the picture of good health, would feel duty-bound to enlighten the family about the latest California food fad; his last dinner topic had been an obscure culinary delight called green magma. Nursing a glass of wine, her father, Doug, would silently eat whatever Laura placed in front of him. He would come to life only when the conversation came around—as it always did—to the family's convenience store franchise business, in which Sarah and her brother had an interest, but the extent of which had never been revealed, despite repeated discreet questions to their father. Doug and Laura would then team up to give an update of the family assets, underscoring their talk with stories and anecdotes about the hard work and acumen required of the two of them. Doug, in particular, prided himself on being the one who ensured the continued abundance they all enjoyed in that competitive market.

There had been another interesting exchange during that New Year's visit, Sarah said. As she and Scott were cleaning up after supper, her mother had come up to her. "Sarah," she had said with a disapproving tone, "I just went to get some fresh kitchen towels, and I just couldn't believe the shape your linen closet is in! I said to Nate, 'You'd think after all these years that your sister would have learned to stack her linens more neatly and with some semblance of order.' You can't find a thing in there!" Nate, who had walked up behind their mother, had smiled sheepishly and spread his arms as if to say, "I give up!" Sarah had had a sense of déjà vu. Not only had her mother criticized her before for the way she kept house—she also remembered a nearly identical scene a decade earlier between Laura, Laura's sister, and *their* mother. That time it had been Laura's closets that had failed to meet maternal standards!

The slice of family life that Sarah recounted to her therapist was fairly representative of what goes on in many families, so it may seem rather tame and undramatic. Yet just as there are glaringly dysfunctional homes, so there are families like Sarah's in which dysfunctional currents and addictive patterns are subtle and run deep, barely rippling the apparently calm and convivial surface of routine interactions. In such settings recurrent themes tend to rise to the surface across generations only in a crisis or when a new element is introduced into the familiar and seemingly manageable tableau.

In observing the family dynamics at her dinner party and in reexamining that experience with her therapist, Sarah, for example, was able to pick out the family's obsession with food (Laura's extra meal, ensuring there would be plenty to eat; Sarah's own cyclical overeating and crash dieting). She also discovered a tradition of controlling matriarchs, as shown by Laura's interference with Sarah's meal planning and, later, her criticism of Sarah's housekeeping, with its crossgenerational echoes.

The visit also confirmed further Sarah's conviction of Doug's problem with drinking. She was aware that he habitually reached for a drink as a coping response to his own feelings, which he was incapable of expressing. There was alcoholism in Doug's family, although it skipped a generation. Doug's father was a teetotaler, perhaps in reaction to his own father's alcoholism. With this history, Doug, his children, and their children are, at the very least, at higher genetic and environmental risk for alcohol dependency.

Finally, Sarah's story also exposed the parental tendency to control others in the family indirectly—through *unilateral decision making, lack of openness,* and the *omission of important information.* Laura neglects to tell Sarah that she is bringing a second meal; Doug fails to tell his children the extent of their family holdings, denying them the autonomy of adulthood and remaining in full control by making business decisions "for their own good." In a way Nate exhibits a subtle symptom of the parental control issues when he colludes with his mother's criticism of Sarah by failing to challenge her about its unfairness. Over the years both Sarah and Nate have learned not to dare risk direct confrontation with their powerful mother.

As you will see later in the chapter, Sarah's powers of observation did not spring up overnight, but were the result of the searching questions she has been asking herself in the course of therapy.

Doug—Sarah and Nate's father—started to work two jobs shortly after Sarah was born. For three years he spent his days starting his franchise business, and most of his evenings stocking vending machines for a salary. After that he expanded his successful start-up business, which in the first few years required an enormous investment of both time and energy.

Although Doug's ambitions were essentially a positive development for the long-term material welfare of the family, the changes in his plans dramatically affected the lives of his wife and children. Laura, lonely and overwhelmed by the sudden responsibility of raising a baby and a five-year-old practically single-handedly, began looking to her son for company. The young child was allowed to stay up later and later at night to keep Mother company, watching the new TV set—possession of which was a symbol of the family's rising fortunes. This special alliance between mother and child, which, ironically, felt very nurturing to Nate at the time, was not healthy for the family as a whole. First of all, it evolved into a kind of collusion. When Doug's car would finally roll into the driveway late at night, Laura would quickly spirit Nate into his bedroom, tucking him in, whispering, "Quick, quick! We mustn't let Daddy know you stayed up so late!" More important, the special alliance created a sort of exclusivity between mother and one child, leaving the other child and the father on the outside. In later years the alliance had its negative side even for Nate. Because of the special companionship her son had offered in those lonely years, Laura continued to see Nate as an extension of herself. Growing up as a very self-sufficient youngster, Nate felt a need to rebel in his teens against the closeness his mother demanded, which had started to feel overprotective.

In any case, Doug never quite returned to the family—either with his physical or his emotional presence. As his business prospered, he became obsessed with his work, addicted to it. Even when he did spend time at home, his presence was not felt in any meaningful way by his family. He had become emotionally distant and withdrawn. Laura continued to be the one in control when it came to family matters. Yet this seeming self-reliance actually covered up her own dependency needs.

In a way this turn of events was not surprising. Doug's own father had died in an automobile accident when Doug had been only four years old. His mother had never remarried, so Doug had had no modeling for male parenting. At some level, therefore, Doug expressed his own discomfort with parenting by finding socially approved ways to distance himself from this role: by "bettering himself" and by competing with single-minded dedication in the professional arena.

Nor did the intergenerational cycle break with Doug. It affected the next generation as well. Once grown, neither of his children had an adequate model to use as a reference when considering a potential mate or possible parenting partner of their unborn children—as attested to by the crises of several divorces and failed committed relationships. For example, Sarah chose two husbands who, on the surface, seemed very different from her father and one another. In fact, however, each in his own way carried on the underlying theme of workaholism masking their emotional unavailability.

HEALTHY FAMILY SYSTEMS

Most of us have a negative response to the word *crisis,* a term that can cause us to feel and act frightened and defeated. We might do better to take our cue from the Chinese, whose symbol for crisis is a compound of two intriguingly different words, *danger* and *opportunity.* In crises as well as in the typical developmental stages of family life, functional families often recognize and experience opportunities for growth, for a new understanding. It is not so much *what* happens in a family, but *how* that family responds to change that shows whether a child is growing up in an environment that is supportive, nurturing, and open—or frightening, inconsistent, chaotic, and confusing. In other words, the extent of a family system's health depends not so much on what challenges it faces, but on the way in which it responds to the challenges that all families face.

If you're like most people who grew up in a dysfunctional home, you may at times have wondered what an optimally functional family might actually look like. One way to look at families is to check how well they have developed six important strengths that have been identified as helping family members survive, learn, and thrive:

1. Commitment to the family, making the family a priority.
2. Emotional/spiritual wellness, allowing trust and the giving and receiving of love.
3. Open communication, with consistent verbal and nonverbal responses.
4. Appreciation and recognition of the positive aspects of otherness.
5. Meaningful time spent together as a family.
6. Ability to deal with conflict and crisis.[1]

A functional family system can also be identified by its rules. In dysfunctional families the rules are characterized by rigidity and inflexibility. By contrast, the healthy family's expectations, values, goals, attitudes, and authority take into consideration human limits and fallibility. This kind of family handles change with flexibility, and its communication patterns encourage openness among its members.[2]

HOW WE REPEAT OUR PARENTS' MISTAKES

In addition to exhibiting these characteristics, the healthy family of origin serves as a blueprint for how to be in the world. Two major issues that people from dysfunctional families struggle with are those dealing with relationships and those dealing with parenting because, as illustrated by Sarah's family, neither one is modeled well in the family of origin. Yet one of the functions of parenting is to model, to be an example to the children. Modeling is so powerful that unless something intervenes, dysfunctions continue to be transmitted from one generation to the next.

Dysfunctional family modeling is grounded in inconsistency and in the double standard—in the old adage, "Do as I say, not as I do." Each of us—children in particular—trusts more what we see than what we hear. Think back to your own childhood. Chances are you'll recall that whenever there was an inconsistency between your mother or father's words and her or his actions, it was the actions that spoke louder. And if her or his behavior was inconsistent from one time to another, or from day to day, you ended up not knowing what to believe about your parent or about yourself. When there is this kind of mismatch, trust is breached. Children grow up confused and unsure of themselves, repeating the endless cycle of dysfunction and, often, of chemical abuse and violence. As adults such people may believe "it will never happen

Sarah's Marriages

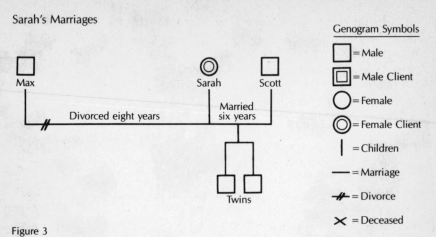

Genogram Symbols

☐ = Male

🔲 = Male Client

◯ = Female

◎ = Female Client

❙ = Children

— = Marriage

⫫ = Divorce

✗ = Deceased

Figure 3

to me" but, in fact, modeling is such a powerful influence that they often recreate in their own lives what they themselves experienced and observed.[3]

Sometimes dysfunctional, crossgenerational family patterns are more easily spotted by drawing what's known as a genogram—a diagram of the relationships among various family members. The one in figure 3 is Sarah's. (Note that it includes a reference to Max, her first husband.)

Some time ago Sarah became concerned about the parenting conflicts she and Scott were having. When she suggested counseling, Scott refused to go. So Sarah decided to consult a psychotherapist on her own. Pointing out that the models for how we parent are rooted in how we, ourselves, were parented, the therapist began by asking Sarah to talk about her family of origin. She explained to Sarah that therapy would help her get in touch with possible unresolved issues from the past, because they have a way of resurfacing years later in current relationships and in the role of parent.

Responding to her therapist's questions about her childhood experiences and memories of interactions with her father, Sarah realized that she had been concerned for a long time about her father's drinking. At first her childhood memories of him were quite sketchy. No one had ever talked about Doug's drinking. Yet once she started searching her memory for clues, Sarah remembered that as a little girl she had been uncomfortable at family celebrations because her dad, usually so quiet and withdrawn, would embarrass her by constantly repeating himself, being boisterous, and acting silly, like someone she didn't know at all. She also began to wonder about the cause of his poor health in recent years—especially about his heart problems and high blood pressure, which had gotten worse lately.

Finally, with encouragement from her therapist and with some trepidation, Sarah summoned the courage to talk to her mother, because she needed support and clarification for her observations. Laura looked at her as if she'd lost her marbles, "What are you talking about? Of course your dad doesn't have a drinking problem. I can't believe that you could even ask such a dumb thing. Where do you get your information, at the beauty shop? A few drinks never hurt anyone—in fact, it's good for you. Haven't you read that doctors now even recommend drinking for people with heart disease?"

But Sarah refused to be sidetracked by her mother's aggressive denial. She had learned that wives and families of alcoholics did not easily let go of their denial that a problem existed, and she was not about to fall into that family trap. Once her suspicions about her father's chemical dependency had been aroused, she did her best to find out more about both her parents' family histories to see if there were clues to alcoholism. She added as much information as she could to her genogram (see figure 4), disappointed that so few of her older relatives were still around to recall previous generations. Striking patterns suddenly became apparent. It was clear that on both her father and her mother's sides of the family, alcoholism was a recurring theme.

Having learned about the genetic and environmental predisposition toward alcoholism, Sarah now realized her own potential vulnerability and high risk for the disease. With guidance from her therapist, however, she was able to evaluate her own drinking behavior and learn that she was not developing a dependence on alcohol. Some of the clues included the fact that she never thought much about her drinking one way or the other. She drank only occasionally, and then very little— usually when she and Scott dined out with friends. She was as likely as not to pick restaurants which did not serve alcohol. Also, she realized she had no interest whatsoever in the home liquor cabinet. It was Scott's job to select the dinner wines when they entertained and to replenish the supplies. (To assess your own drinking pattern, please refer to the Appendix 2 questionnaire. To assess other addictive behaviors, see Appendices 3 through 9.)

On the other hand, in the process of reexamining her relationship with her father and with other men with whom she had been in relationship, Sarah recognized that she had her own form of addiction. She got her fix from men rather than from an addictive substance, but the dynamics were the same. She had learned that an addictive process underlies all addictions and that a test of addiction is not so much whether a person can "white-knuckle it" to stay away from the addictive trigger, but what happens once she or he is engaged with it.

Regardless of the addiction—whether it's to alcohol, compulsive overeating, another person, or any other addictive stimulus—once engaged with it, addicts cannot or will not stop, even when the behavior is clearly causing problems in their social, family, or work life. Sarah knew her past relationship patterns fit this criterion of addiction. With this new understanding, Sarah began to wonder about other addiction patterns besides alcoholism that might

Sarah's Family History

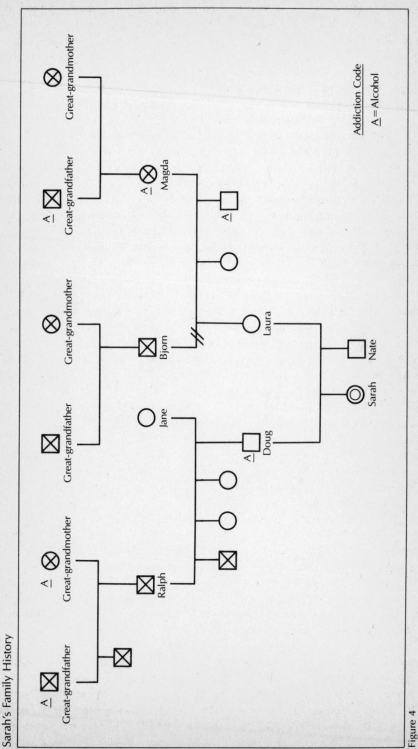

Addiction Code

A = Alcohol

Figure 4

emerge from her family genogram. Now that she knew that most people prone to the addictive process tended to choose partners with complementary addictions, she also became curious about her own mate selection process. For some time she had been uneasy about Scott's seeming need to be constantly busy, but for the first time she recognized its compulsive pattern, one more meaningful piece of this intergenerational family puzzle. By the time she decided to extend her genogram to include Max, her first husband, she was not overly surprised to find that he too came from an addiction-prone family.[4] (See figure 5 for this extended genogram.)

Sarah's process of discovery was fairly typical. Although awareness is certainly a long way from changing one's behavior, at least Sarah was now in a position to break the crossgenerational pattern by making choices different from those made in the past and by educating her own children, alerting them to their family predisposition toward addictions.

Even though Scott continued to overwork, Sarah started taking better care of her own needs. She joined Al-Anon, a Twelve-Step group for families and friends of alcoholics. She continued individual psychotherapy and joined a women's group for relationship addicts. There she began to deal with her own co-dependent responses to a workaholic husband and an emotionally unavailable ex-husband, which were rooted in her own family's history. She also began monitoring herself daily for signs of slips into addictive behaviors. (Appendix 10 is her checklist of questions.)

WHAT OUR FAMILY TEACHES US ABOUT RELATIONSHIPS

In addition to modeling parenting, another particularly important modeling function of parents is to show how to be in relationship with an intimate partner. Although the willingness of any family member to be open and vulnerable with her or his feelings can create a sense of connectedness and closeness, true intimacy is more than closeness. It can occur only between peers—that is, where there is a balance of power.

QUALITIES OF INTIMACY

The qualities that people often associate with intimacy are trust, safety, acceptance, and openness. But three additional key ingredients are needed before a relationship can be described as intimate: mutuality, reciprocal empathy, and a balance of power. Among other things, mutuality reflects the choice two people make to be with one another, which also implies its opposite: each can choose to leave. Empathy speaks to the willingness of each person to enter the subjective world of the partner in order to better understand and feel the other's experience.

Sarah's Extended Genogram

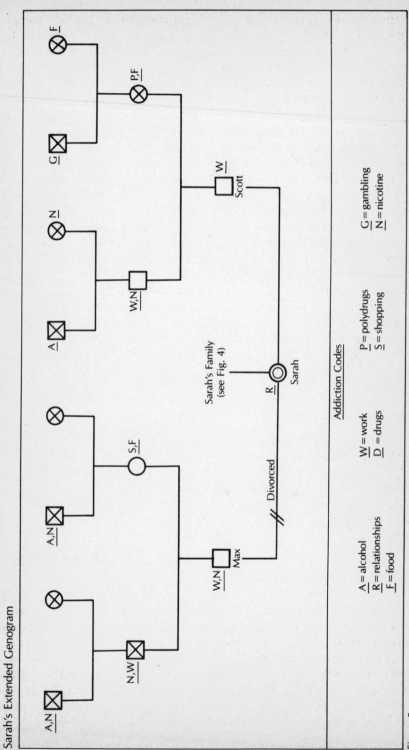

Addiction Codes

A = alcohol	W = work	P = polydrugs	G = gambling
R = relationships	D = drugs	S = shopping	N = nicotine
F = food			

Figure 5

Once we include mutuality and reciprocal empathy in the criteria for intimacy, however, we realize that early childhood relationships with adults, albeit quite close, can never be intimate. Because a child is dependent on adults for survival, he or she cannot choose to leave—thus precluding mutuality. And because his or her experience and emotional range are limited, a child cannot enter the subjective world of the adult—thus precluding reciprocal empathy.

In other words, for intimacy to unfold, there must be a balance of power. Therefore, given that adults and children cannot be peers, what children experience with their parents, even in healthy families, is closeness, not intimacy. At best, intimacy can only be modeled *by* parents *for* children.

Realistically, we all know that even adults are not always equal. Especially if you're older than thirty five, you will find few men and women of your parents' generation who have been equals in their relationships with one another; power between them has rarely been balanced—either from a psychological or a socioeconomic point of view. Yet your parents have been your primary models for intimacy and for how to be a woman or a man in the world. How they were with one another when you were a child has been indelibly imprinted on you.

Another time when adults are not equals is when they are in an addictive relationship. When people feel they are dependent on another for survival, they are no longer able to choose to leave. When they give up their freedom to choose, they give up their personal power. Essentially they become childlike, precluding the possibility of intimacy. So, in fact, for relationship addicts, intimacy is the gift of recovery.

In expanding her family's genogram, Sarah gained a better understanding of her mother and father. Neither Laura nor Doug had received positive modeling for parenting or intimacy in their own families of origin. Laura, Sarah's mother, had been raised in a strict and emotionally distant home in Norway, whose family motto, proudly emblazoned on the leaded-glass family shield, was *Ora et Labora*—pray and work. She never received a compliment or word of encouragement for being an honor student and an outstanding violinist; this was considered the minimum acceptable family standard. Transactions among family members were formal and cold. Laura could not recall ever being asked to share her feelings, or receiving a warm hug as a youngster, except occasionally from her father. He did not stay to see her grow into adulthood, however; when she was eleven he filed for divorce.

FATHER HUNGER

Even after she had become an adult and had raised her own daughters, Laura would find herself still trying to please her mother, hoping to get the approval she was certain would be forthcoming if only she would be a better person. And, as shown by the negative effect that the early loss of his father had on Doug's later relationships, it is clear that men also suffer from lack of modeling for intimacy. Having lost a father only magnifies what in our society has been an all too typical male experience. Many contemporary men think of their fathers' world as having been very remote from their own and their mothers'—a world that was abstract, unreal for them, and far from intimate. Men who grew up with such typical American fathers—physically present but *psychologically* absent—often suffer from "father hunger," "a subconscious yearning for an ideal father that results in behavior ranging from self-pity to hypermasculinity and frustrates attempts to achieve intimacy."[5]

As Andrew Merton has written, the effects of father hunger can be devastating.

The main business of the father's life was not here with the family, but somewhere else, somewhere outside, where life was played out in a broader sphere, which in his son's imagination was much more fascinating, much more exciting. But intimacy is not something that can be learned from an abstraction. And this is why father hunger tends to be passed from generation to generation—why the son of a father-hungry father will be father hungry himself. . . . For a man who fails to develop an intimate relationship with his wife has an extremely poor chance of doing so with his children.[6]

Our society's paradigm for how to be a man has come from the long-approved and familiar image of the hard-working achiever in the business world—competent, competitive, out of touch with his feelings, preoccupied with material success, positively reinforced for conforming, for being tough, for being "one of the boys," for putting business first.

Sarah realized that Max, her former husband, fit this image. At first, she was comfortable with Max because he was so much like her father. She felt attracted to his sense of responsibility, competence, and ambition. To her, Max seemed as solid as the Rock of Gibraltar. But soon she realized that, just like her own father, Max was also emotionally distant and often unavailable. His apparent inability to be close was the predictable outcome of lack of positive modeling for intimacy in his family. His father had died when Max was fourteen. When, as the oldest of five children, Max was forced to take on the role of substitute father he did his best to emulate his father's stereotypic parenting style and "all-American male" image.

MOTHER AS ROLE MODEL

Women, of course, are also profoundly influenced by their fathers. For them, however, the most frequent socially acceptable model has been transmitted by a mother who was a traditional homemaker. Such mothers spent many years attending to the needs of their husbands and children, self-sacrificing, always subordinating their needs to those of others, made to feel guilty by their family and society if they dared display any restlessness, dissatisfaction, or—God forbid—selfishness. Sarah quipped that in the early days, when her parents were still struggling, her mother was such a caretaker for her father that she would not only get up every morning to fix him his lunch, she would suck the air out of the plastic sandwich bag to ensure freshness!

Our approved social model for relationship is one that often brings together an emotionally handicapped, fiercely masculine male and a servant sensitive to his every need. Although this may sound like an exaggeration, it is based on the experience of many couples. When boys and girls grow up in model American families, they bring intimacy problems to their own adult relationships—yet another example of crossgenerational influence.

If these are society's models for relationship, it is not difficult to imagine what the outcomes are when an overlay of family dysfunction is superimposed on them. Take a woman who grows up with a mother who is mentally ill or alcoholic, or a woman who has felt the pressure to match up to the energy, drive, power, and control of a supermom such as Sarah's mother—how will these experiences affect the daughter's perception of women's roles?

DYSFUNCTIONAL FAMILIES

As illustrated by Sarah's life, dysfunctional families are inadequate in two fundamental ways:

- On the one hand, they model behaviors and responses that are unhealthy, undesirable, self-devaluing, or inappropriate;
- Conversely, they *fail* to model behaviors and responses that are healthy, desirable, self-enhancing, and appropriate.

Recently a client narrowly missed hitting a man at a crosswalk while she was driving. Even though she was deeply shaken by the experience, when she got home she recounted the incident to her husband as if it were a big joke. Her husband didn't quite know how to react, so he laughed with her. This made the woman feel misunderstood and discounted, and soon they were enmeshed in an argument.

This story is a good illustration of the communication problems that inappropriate modeling can cause. This client grew up in a family where the father was alcoholic. She had more negative interaction with her mother than with her father, something that is not uncommon, because the alcoholic's spouse (referred to as "co-dependent" or "co-alcoholic") is usually the more visible, active, and controlling parent. Partly because of women's socialization, a co-dependent often also feels powerless and acts like a martyr or victim, creating a climate of tension and guilt in the children. As a result of this setting, it was the mother's role modeling that profoundly affected the child in a negative way.

Whenever, as a little girl, this woman hurt herself, her mother would make light of it and just laugh about it—an extension of having learned to avoid facing the seriousness and sadness of their lives. Her mother's response was not selective: no matter what the extent of the child's physical or emotional trauma, it was always greeted by laughter.

Today this client's own automatic response to hurtful or embarrassing situations is to laugh. Given her dysfunctional style of communication, it would be difficult for any partner to know how to accurately read or respond to a message. In this particular case things were made worse by the fact that the client's husband is himself from a dysfunctional family. Typical of adults of his background, he is a high monitor of others' moods, taking his cues from them for how to react. Therefore when his wife laughed, it came natural to him to just follow suit—not allowing his own feelings to let him know that laughter was inappropriate to the situation.

QUALITIES THAT HELP BUILD HEALTHY FAMILIES

Every family system and every relationship has its own unique character and special features. Yet just as there are common symptoms of family dysfunction, so people growing up in functional homes share certain common experiences that seem to be essential for growing up into healthy, responsible, and well-balanced social beings.

Connectedness

Connectedness is a feeling of closeness, of being an integral part of the family, of having a sense of solidarity and cohesion with the other members. Connectedness is the opposite of alienation, isolation. When they feel connected at home, children learn a sense of rootedness and community and are more likely to see themselves as relational beings at ease in the world's social network.

In Sarah's family those most likely to feel a sense of deep connection are Laura and Nate, because Laura, the mother, out of her own needs, established an especially close connection with Nate when he was quite young. But because this connection excluded both the father and the younger sister, it did not foster family connectedness.

Acceptance

To accept means to acknowledge, respect, and honor the uniqueness of each family member. A child who feels that differences are accepted in the family develops greater self-confidence and self-esteem, and has a better chance of realizing his or her potential.

When Sarah was growing up, her parents were very accepting of the fact that academically she did not excel to the same degree as her brother. They went to great lengths to support Sarah's athletic abilities, and to ensure she would have an opportunity to do well in that arena. By the time she was in eleventh grade, Sarah had become a top-seeded junior golfer in their area.

On another level this kind of acceptance might be considered somewhat ambiguous. In situations like this one, it is impossible to know whether the motivation was one of pure acceptance or whether it was partly a reflection of ambitious parents' needs to have all their children excel. For Sarah the experience was very positive. In addition to being rewarding for its own sake, golf was a sport that the family enjoyed together, so Sarah had the opportunity to spend time with her father when she otherwise would not have.

Appreciation

Family members need to be acknowledged for their personal successes and for their contributions to the family. Families that appreciate how every member does his or her share run a lesser risk of taking contributions for granted, and contributors are less likely to feel used or exploited.

Often the one least appreciated is the mother who dedicates her life to her family. The father usually takes the accolades, because he makes the most tangible contribution. Because he understands tangible contributions best, he is typically also the first to take his homemaker wife for granted—modeling a dysfunctional dynamic for the children.

Trust

Trust develops slowly. In the family children learn to trust those who are consistent, reasonable, predictable, forgiving, respectful, and loving toward them, and at least consistent, reasonable, and respectful toward others with whom they have dealings—whether the relationships are personal, social, or professional. As children we may *like* someone who treats us better than someone else, but at the deepest core of our being we *trust* that person only if she or he deals fairly with everyone.

Sarah and Nate, for example, are closer to their mother, but they tend to place their trust in their father. Despite the fact that he is rather withdrawn and distant, Doug is experienced by his children as being at least more consistent and predictable than their mother.

Truthfulness

Truthfulness has to do not only with the important information or feelings we share, but also with those we omit. Denial is a major type of lie that clouds dysfunctional families. It is the dissonance between the way things are and the way the family says or believes they are. Denial is truly devastating to a child's development. Growing up surrounded by denial makes people unable to deal with reality and incapable of identifying and trusting their feelings and judgment.

Families can foster an atmosphere of truthfulness by establishing a safe environment, an environment in which family members feel free to question and free to express their views and their feelings without threat of judgment or ridicule.

Recall that when Sarah questioned her mother about her father's alcoholism, her mother not only denied it, but chose a sarcastic, caustic style to silence Sarah.

Commitment

Family members who commit to the family have chosen to make the family a priority in their lives. They are people on whom the family can rely. Being committed to the family means taking the time and making the effort to spend quality time with them, to carefully build relationships, and to work through problems with mutual caring and respect.

Doug's commitment to his family was limited; it basically consisted of ensuring the financial well-being of the family. His lack of deeper commitment was betrayed by the fact that he would not spend time with Sarah as a youngster except when it entailed something of personal interest to him, such as golf.

Flexible rules

Change is one of the few certainties in life—yet it brings uncertainty in its wake. Dysfunctional families, fearful of the loss of control implied by the uncertainties of change, often try to enforce an unnatural stability onto unstable situations.

Inflexible rules are a reflection of this desire to control and are another form of denial, because they deny the reality that things and people are constantly changing. Optimal families, on the other hand, operate not by rules but by negotiation based on values. They tend to take a collaborative problem-solving approach to change—focusing more on the opportunity aspect of crisis than on its danger.

People who grow up in overly rigid families tend to go to one or the other extreme in their own adult lives—they may rebel against rules even when they are reasonable, or they may continue leading their own lives with a lack of adaptability that precludes healthy personal and relational growth.

Over the past year, Sarah has maintained a rigid 7 P.M. bedtime for the twins. In therapy, she realized that, in effect, she was carrying on her own family's inflexibility, reinforced by her mother's rigid rules. With this insight Sarah learned that she can parent in a different way—for example, by keeping the basic 7 P.M. time, but feeling free to make changes when there is a special TV show or family celebration.

Problem-solving skills

An important function of the members of a healthy family, especially of the parents, is the modeling of good thinking skills. A family that is in denial, where people are not free and safe to be themselves, is dealing with such distortions that healthy thinking and problem solving become impossible. The healthy family, on the other hand, uses its connectedness, its trust, and its flexibility to help its members come to the most appropriate decision in any situation, and to identify and accept the likely consequences of that decision.

By being overly trusting with a fellow student she barely knew, a college freshman client recently ended up losing her entire month's food and rent allowance. When, in dismay, she called her father for assistance, he neither jumped in to solve the problem for her nor grilled her or criticized her. Being a reasonable parent, he knew that there would be time to ask for details later. Besides, he realized events had already taught her the lesson she needed to learn. Instead he calmed her down, helped her to identify all her options, and then supported her when she made her decision. He was very careful not to make the decision for her, not wanting to foster dependence on himself.

Safety

It is impossible to separate safety from trust. No trust can develop without people feeling safe, nor can people feel safe when they can't trust. Many kinds of safety are needed in a family if a child is to grow up self-confident and willing to take reasonable risks. A child must be safe from verbal, emotional, physical, and sexual abuse; from being treated like a scapegoat; from being expected to take on roles, work, or responsibilities that are unreasonable for her or his age and position. And a child must feel safe to disagree openly and to make mistakes.

Sarah did not feel safe to set limits with her mother because she was afraid to test whether she was accepted unconditionally as a separate individual. In order for her to risk building intimate and lasting relationships later in life, she needed not only positive parental modeling, but also a sense of being heard, understood, and accepted for who she was.

Boundaries

A personal boundary is the edge between one person and another— where the first person stops and the other begins. A boundary can also be visualized as a space bubble that surrounds a person. Relationship addicts often find it difficult to respect others' boundaries because, having a weak sense of self, they are unsure of their own boundaries. Children growing up in a dysfunctional family with a mother who is a relationship addict often experience her as very intrusive. Even though such children may be unable to verbalize these feelings, they sense that their personal boundary or space bubble is being violated. Yet because of the imbalance of power, children are unable to protect themselves. In reaction, such a child may grow up filled with rage and frustration, shutting down emotionally whenever anyone tries to get close.

In a healthy family, on the other hand, the parents' own boundaries are well defined. The chances that they will recognize and respect the children's separateness and individuality are much greater. Such children grow up feeling they have a whole range of choices in relating to others—from intimacy to casual acquaintance—and they feel comfortable setting reasonable limits accordingly.

Intrusiveness is perhaps one of the most common boundary issues in families. Depending on the degree of the family's dysfunction, it can range widely—from reading people's mail, to eavesdropping, to various forms of abuse.

It has often been said that we live in a narcissistic age. Put simply, to be narcissistic means to be wrapped up in yourself, to have an inflated self-concept, and to view others as being there to serve and enhance your life. In other words, people with narcissistic traits see others as extensions of themselves, and in this sense narcissism is another boundary issue—one that is present in many dysfunctional homes.

Narcissistic boundary issues were a recurring theme in Sarah's family. Although all mothers are pleased when people fuss over their babies, Laura's delight with compliments paid to her firstborn, Nate, bordered on the narcissistic, because she used them to enhance her own self-esteem. It was as though anything that happened to Nate happened only in relation to herself, almost as if he did not have a separate existence. As Nate got older, Laura pushed her very bright son into academic competition, casually dropping remarks about his IQ and his outstanding school performance to her friends—as if he were just another of her successful projects, rather than a unique and separate person who deserved most of the credit for his achievements.

From time to time Nate now shows these self-centered traits himself. When, some time ago, his own son quietly announced that he wanted to change from his private middle school to the local junior high, Nate was shocked and angry. His first reaction wasn't concern for his son's feelings or curiosity about this sudden decision. All Nate could think about was the negative effect the change might have on his own and his family's social status. His response was, "How could you do this to me, knowing how much it would upset me!"

EXERCISES: YOUR FAMILY OF ORIGIN

EXERCISE I: YOUR FAMILY'S ATTITUDES AND BEHAVIOR

The exercise that follows lists the qualities of healthy families, discussed in the preceding section. To what extent were these traits present in your family of origin? To what extent are you recreating that environment in your marriage or other important relationships?

A *1* is the lowest mark, indicating the relative absence of a trait; a *10* is the highest, indicating the relative presence of each trait.

1. Circle the number on the scale that shows how you would rate your parents/family during your childhood—preferably during the time when you were between the ages of three and seven; if possible, make your rating based on *specific* incidents you recall.
2. Now go back and on each scale place a star where your relationship behavior as an adult fits any one of the ten factors. Before rating yourself, it is important for you to spend some time in reviewing, as honestly as you can, specific situations and incidents in your recent past, so that your rating will be based on your *actions*, not merely on what you feel or believe.
3. Next, place an arrow at the place on each scale where you would like to be in your relationship. Be realistic—don't try to make such huge leaps that you'll feel discouraged and quit when you realize that the goals you set are beyond your reach at this time.
4. Finally, from the ten factors, choose one to make your top priority for change over the next ninety days. List in sequence the *observable* activities and steps it will take to get to where you want to be from where you are now. *Observable* means that for each activity you write down, you should be able to answer the question, What behaviors of mine can serve as indicators that I am moving toward my goal? Again, a word of caution: don't overdo; be satisfied with modest progress. A path is built one step at a time.

For example, in piecing together her relationship history since high school, Sarah realized that she had always been so readily available to men that she would routinely cancel previous plans with her girlfriends when a chance for a date with her current heartthrob would suddenly come up. Over the years this carelessness had caused her to lose all but her most tolerant friends. On taking a closer look at her present behavior, Sarah was horrified to discover that, even now, she would make plans with her two closest friends only when Scott was out of town.

She decided to commit to seeing each of these friends at least twice a month—regardless of Scott's travel schedule. A positive indicator for her was the fact that last month she kept a date with one of her friends, even though Scott had come home unexpectedly with a pair of tickets to see one of their favorite comedy teams.

Lowest   Highest

1. Connectedness

| 1 | 2 | 3 | 4 | 5 | 6 | 7 | 8 | 9 | 10 |

2. Acceptance

| 1 | 2 | 3 | 4 | 5 | 6 | 7 | 8 | 9 | 10 |

3. Appreciation

| 1 | 2 | 3 | 4 | 5 | 6 | 7 | 8 | 9 | 10 |

4. Trust

| 1 | 2 | 3 | 4 | 5 | 6 | 7 | 8 | 9 | 10 |

5. Truthfulness

| 1 | 2 | 3 | 4 | 5 | 6 | 7 | 8 | 9 | 10 |

6. Commitment

| 1 | 2 | 3 | 4 | 5 | 6 | 7 | 8 | 9 | 10 |

7. Flexible Rules

| 1 | 2 | 3 | 4 | 5 | 6 | 7 | 8 | 9 | 10 |

8. Problem-Solving Skills

| 1 | 2 | 3 | 4 | 5 | 6 | 7 | 8 | 9 | 10 |

9. Safety

| 1 | 2 | 3 | 4 | 5 | 6 | 7 | 8 | 9 | 10 |

10. Boundaries

| 1 | 2 | 3 | 4 | 5 | 6 | 7 | 8 | 9 | 10 |

EXERCISE II: YOUR RELATIONSHIP WITH YOUR PARENTS

So far we have focused primarily on the family system, on parental modeling, and on identifiable characteristics of functional and dysfunctional homes. In reading this chapter and in doing the previous exercise, you have undoubtedly come up with memories of particular scenes from your childhood—some involving siblings, some grandparents, and many of them your parents. These, however, are mere glimpses into your interactions with your mother and father.

You may find that the Relationship History Chart (figure 6) can help you to round out the picture, deepening your understanding of your overall relationship with your mother and father and of what someone has called "our inevitable disappointment with parents."

Save the completed chart. You will have a chance to refer to it later when we look at patterns and connections between past and present. For now, you'll probably find it helpful to write or record on tape the feelings you experienced in working on this assigment.

Even though opening up ourselves to the past is necessary if we want to better understand the present, usually it is also a very painful process. Some people find huge gaps in their childhood memories, others are overwhelmed with too much information from their families or too many memories. Share your feelings and insights with someone who supports you and cares about you, especially if you find that certain information or memories are difficult for you to deal with alone.

Some wit has said, "The truth will set you free, but first it will make you miserable." Keep in mind that the discomfort you may be experiencing in reopening closed chapters of your life has an important function. Before we can make changes, we must find out what changes need to be made. The impulse to change invariably begins with pain . . . which leads to awareness.

Relationship History Chart

	1. Mother		2. Father		3.		4.		5.		6.		
Characteristics of relationship													
Character-istics of person													
My role, my feelings													
Rewards of relationship													
Prices of relationship													
Involvement w/chemicals or other addictive behaviors													
Response to addictive behaviors													

Figure 6
Source: Sue Evans, L.P., Minneapolis, MN.

CHAPTER 3

The Enchanted Garden: Rediscovering Your Inner Child

PAULA

Paula was living on the edge when she first surrendered to the idea that she might need psychotherapy. Her appearance was deceptive. She was a pale wisp of a woman in her early thirties, almost childlike in appearance. Yet in the two years since completing her medical residency, she had already built up a very busy and thriving private practice working with a senior associate. In her spare time she saw patients at a community clinic three times a week and team taught a course at a medical school.

Her fingernails bitten to the quick, the restlessness of her hands, and the tension in her face and body betrayed the frantic pace she led and the extreme stress she experienced. Her presence in the therapist's office wasn't her idea, she said; she had always been quite self-sufficient and able to handle her own problems. She explained that this session was the culmination of a series of current stresses both at home and at work. Two patients and the office receptionist in recent months had complained to her associate about her gruffness. Her relationship with the man she had been living with for the past two years had deteriorated. He had reverted to spending much of his time with his former wife and the children from that marriage. He and her friends were also contributing to her stress by "badgering" her about her recent weight loss, which she brushed aside as an ordinary fluctuation, "nothing to be concerned about."

According to Paula, her problems were due to a temporary situation. She had recently been spending practically every free moment—of which she admittedly had very few—preparing for her board certification exams. The pressure to pass them had been tremendous. She had already failed them once, and not passing would jeopardize her teaching, her private practice, and her overall career plans. But the physician she shared her practice with had seen the problem differently. A few weeks earlier, after Paula had taken the exams, she had given her an ultimatum: enter psychotherapy or end their professional association. While Paula had pondered her next move, she had been notified that she had failed the board exams again. That had been the last straw.

She was in a box, Paula said. She felt exhausted, drained. The stress had become so intense that she had nearly fainted while driving on the freeway the previous day. She knew that what she really needed was relief from the stress and the physical and emotional exhaustion and anxiety; yet there was no place where she could cut back. Her boyfriend, her professional associate, her students, and the patients at the clinic all depended on her, relied on her strength. She couldn't possibly let those people down. And because she, as a physician, felt she knew all about stress, she also questioned what contribution psychotherapy could make to her situation.

Paula's problems turned out to be much more severe and of longer standing than she was willing to admit to herself or her therapist. She identified stress as the problem, because it was the symptom that was least threatening to her self-image as a superwoman who had no imperfections or unmet emotional needs. For, in fact, when she started psychotherapy, she had both an addiction problem and a very serious eating disorder. It turned out that she had been abusing alcohol to reduce the tension, "speed" to counteract the exhaustion, and diuretics and laxatives to correct what she saw as her chronic tendency to "get fat"—a totally unrealistic self-image that did not match her frail, emaciated appearance. Her concern about weight gain was one symptom of a case of anorexia so serious that for a time Paula's life was in jeopardy. And the crisis that brought her to therapy was an awesome demonstration of the power a neglected inner child can have over even the most strong-willed individualist.

THE WOUNDED ADULT

Paula was the only child of wealthy parents—both actively alcoholic during her childhood. They adored her. When they were sober they showered the young child with caring attention, affection, and treats. At such times she felt really special. At other times, during and after their periodic drinking binges, she felt completely ignored and neglected. Her very first memory of her parents, retrieved under hypnosis, was of such an incident, when she was barely two and still in a crib. Her parents had taken her to the beach. The day had been filled with joy—the three of them splashing in the surf and collecting colorful pebbles and other treasures. That night her father tucked her in with a big hug while her mother softly hummed a lullaby, stroking her hair until Paula drifted contentedly into slumber. But when she awoke the next morning, happy and eager to get up, no one came when she called. With increasing frustration and rage she yelled and cried for what seemed like hours, rattling the bars of her crib to get her parents' attention. Eventually Paula had drifted off into a fitful sleep—uncomfortable in her soiled diapers, hungry, exhausted, and, above all, confused.

Because of her parents' dramatically inconsistent behavior, Paula grew up very needy and unable to ever trust her reality. As a child she had interpreted her parents' behavior as an unspoken message that she was not worthy of their care and love. The inconsistent care she had received had also made her despise being dependent on others and contemptuous of the part of herself that still had infantile needs. In reaction, she made it a point to seem very independent, needing nothing from anyone—a real superwoman. She met some of her own unfulfilled, disowned needs unconsciously by projecting them onto her patients and boyfriend, convincingly telling herself, "I can't let them down; they really need me."

Denying her dependence created problems for Paula especially in her primary relationship. Her partner was twenty years her senior. In many ways he was a substitute father from whom she demanded perfect empathy, constant reassurance, and immediate availability. With such unrealistic expectations, the inevitable disappointments that followed such demands triggered her painful early childhood experience. At such times Paula would become plaintive and manipulative. With an injured air designed to produce guilt in him she would complain, "I ask so little, and you can't even do that much for me!"

A central issue for Paula lay in her inability to accept and nurture herself. At an unconscious level she did everything in her power to negate her inner needs—to the point of nearly dying of starvation because she refused to feed herself. Sadly, just as she had been emotionally abused in her childhood, so she was abusive to herself as an adult. She lived a life filled with paradoxes: externally an independent contemporary woman, internally an emotionally deprived little girl afraid to grow up. Trained to be a competent healer, she was incompetent to manage her own wholeness, denying her own profound wounds until it was nearly too late.

After spending more than a month in a hospital to treat her anorexia and chemical dependency, Paula began the slow, painful process of reevaluating her early experiences in the family and of learning to care for herself—the prospects that held the most immediate promise of bridging the early separation of her inner child and her adult self.

YOUR INNER CHILD

A little child is hidden within each of us. The theme of the inner child has been explored by a number of clinicians and theorists since the mid-1940s.[1] In the past decade the theme of the "child within" has been picked up most prominently by the self-help group Adult Children of Alcoholics (ACA)—and with good reason. Children who were raised in dysfunctional homes often grow up in a wounded child state. And, as adults, the sense of deprivation is so deeply buried, its insistent call often goes unrecognized. Instead people seek quick emotional fixes that drown it out.

Often when we think of childhood wounds, we think only of physical or sexual abuse, where the traumas are more evident. But the implications of emotional wounding may be equally important for a person's wholeness. Emotional wounding can take place not only when a child's *outer* needs are not met, but also when the *inner* needs are ignored or neglected. This may be more likely to happen out of parental ignorance—that is, lack of knowledge, understanding, or awareness—than out of neglect. Also the parents themselves may have been abused or wounded as children, so unless a crisis or a major intervention takes place to break the pattern, they perpetuate the only model they know into the next generation, in an endless cycle of dysfunctional family dynamics. This pattern of multigenerational transmission fits Paula's family. Her mother, for example, had wealthy parents who traveled all over the world when she was a child, frequently leaving her with household staff. Much of the time Paula was also left with a nanny, a caring woman who was inconsistent in meeting the young child's physical and emotional needs because of her many other household responsibilities. Therefore, although Paula's mother was not abused in the common sense of the word, the repeated separations from her parents without an adequate substitute were wounding experiences. Without the benefit of other models, she was bound to repeat the familiar pattern in raising Paula. Her drinking then aggravated a family pattern that was fundamentally dysfunctional.

Even with poor starts, we are capable of meeting many of our own needs. Honoring, nurturing, and healing—in effect, reparenting—our wounded inner child can help us overcome our feelings of inadequacy and dependence, learning again to feel, play, be joyful and creative. Paula's own emotional depletion contributed to both her personal and professional burnout—you can't share a drink of water when your own cup is empty.

HUMAN SURVIVAL NEEDS

When we talk of "basic survival needs" we are usually speaking of food, water, sleep, and shelter—the bare essentials the body needs in the life-or-death crisis of someone lost in the wilderness. While it is common for the basic survival needs of children growing up in high-stress families not to be met, in order for infants to thrive, and even to merely survive, their psychological and emotional needs must also receive attention.

More than forty years ago, researchers coined the phrase *hospitalism* to describe their observations of institutionalized infants. Even though the infants' physical needs were adequately met, an alarming number of them simply wasted away and died.

What's more, as anthropologist Ashley Montagu observes, that the failure of infants to thrive seemed to occur in the home as well:

It was found to occur quite often among babies in the "best" homes, hospitals, and institutions, among those babies apparently receiving the best and most careful *physical* [italics ours] attention. It became apparent that babies in the poorest homes, with a good mother, despite the lack of hygienic physical conditions, often overcame the physical handicaps and flourished. What was wanting in the sterilized environment of the babies of the first [group] and was generously supplied to babies of the second [group] was mother love.[2]

Similarly, a study with newborn rhesus monkeys found that contact comfort was more important to the infants than nursing comfort. Given a choice of two mother surrogates—one made of bare wire, the other covered with soft fabric—the infants spent overwhelmingly more time with the cloth-covered "mother," even when she was not attached to a nursing device, during five months of observation. The research team concluded that "the primary function of nursing as an affectional variable is that of insuring frequent and intimate body contact of the infant with the mother. . . . We may be sure there is nothing to be gained by giving lip service to love."[3] Caring touch, then, is also a basic human need—basic for wholesome growth.

UNMET NEEDS

The unmet needs of adults who grew up in dysfunctional homes are often not as obvious and clear-cut as the cases just described. Their survival into adulthood attests to the fact that their basic physical needs must have been met much of the time. As in the case of Paula, their emotional and psychological needs may also have been met, at least fitfully and minimally—either by the primary caretaker, usually the mother, or through the nurturance of others in the extended family, such as grandparents, older siblings, uncles and aunts, or even nannies.

Children whose needs are not met spontaneously by others often find unhealthy, seemingly effective ways to meet their own. According to "stroke economy" theory,[4] children who don't receive enough positive strokes begin to settle for negative strokes rather than get no strokes at all. (Originally used to refer to physical touching, the definition of stroking has been extended to include any act that implies the recognition of another's presence.) Nothing is worse than being completely ignored. This kind of sensory and emotional deprivation, or recognition hunger, threatens and places into question a person's very existence. There is truth in the saying, "The opposite of love is not hate, but indifference."

So children who receive no attention and affection from their parents often begin to "act out," unconsciously seeking the attention they so desperately need to survive—even if it means being yelled at, or receiving a spanking or some more severe form of punishment. For children in some families, punishment unfortunately escalates into violence. Amazingly, children who are abused by a parent continue to remain bonded to that parent. Attendants in children's wards report that children hospitalized as a result of severe physical parental abuse still cry at night for that parent.

Unless new learning intervenes, children who are used to negative strokes continue to act out similar scenarios in their adulthood. It is the only way they know of getting attention. Partly because of feelings of low self-worth, at some level they have convinced themselves that punishment is what they deserve. Not only do people raised with negative strokes often enter into abusive primary relationships, they often stay in them, even when their sanity and life are at risk. But relationship dysfunction is only one of the ways in which woundedness manifests in adulthood. Chemical dependency, depressions, anxiety, phobias, self-mutilating behavior (such as cutting or burning oneself), eating disorders, and prostitution are some of the others.

MARCIA

Marcia, today a woman in her late twenties, grew up in a so-called good home, where she received mostly negative strokes. She was the youngest of four siblings. Her father was a high-ranking military officer—a strict authoritaran who ran the family like his idea of an army platoon, on a strict punishment-and-reward system. In this family punishment was always meted out by the father. Although it was not what is usually defined as abuse, nevertheless Marcia remembers it as severe, cruel, and also frightening because of her father's dispassionate efficiency. Other options for shaping the children's behavior (such as rewards for desired behavior and the taking away of privileges for undesirable behavior or using "time outs") were never considered.

Because the family moved a number of times due to the father's reassignments, it was difficult for Marcia to make friends. As she grew older breaking into established peer groups at new schools became increasingly difficult. Not realizing that this was a normal outcome of the frequent moves to new areas, Marcia personalized the situation, becoming more insecure. She blamed herself for being excluded, believing herself to be the proverbial ugly duckling misfit among the young swans. She felt powerless and insecure, and developed a great need to hold onto whatever she could—whether things or people—that might provide the sense of stability she craved.

Eager to break away, at age eighteen Marcia married the first man who proposed. She immediately had a baby, determined to create for herself the family stability she had never experienced. It was during her pregnancy, as stress increased between her and her husband, that he first slapped her. Marcia dismissed this event as unimportant, and "probably my fault. I pushed him too hard." But physical violence is seldom an isolated incident. Predictably the assaults increased in frequency and escalated in degree of violence. Marcia now blamed the battering on his drinking. Even when she was battered to the point of having to be hospitalized, it was not enough to make her leave. She finally left for the first time the night her husband hit her while she held their son in her arms. Her own safety had not been worth protecting, she had felt, but her child's was. Marcia went back to her husband several times. Only through psychotherapy and other interventions was she able to overcome her self-blame and deep feelings of worthlessness to the point of having the strength to leave permanently. Her responses were typical of the "battered wife syndrome." The seemingly unexplainable inability of women to leave what, to all the world, is a clearly abusive and dangerous situation is rooted in the low self-esteem common to abusive families.

WHAT HAPPENED TO *YOUR* UNMET NEEDS?

Whenever as children we are confronted with very painful or frightening experiences, we tend to internalize, or "stuff," them. This is especially true of an infant's first two years of life, because during that time the child has no language or conceptual labels to attach to the feelings it experiences. Unresolved feelings of frustration, fear, and rage that surround a young child's unmet needs for nurturance and caring are often internalized. They may remain unconscious into adulthood, when the state of woundedness finds expression in unexpected ways in relationships. By age two Paula had already stuffed her frustration and rage, learning that her parents couldn't be counted on. Later, she interpreted her early experience as cause and effect: if her parents weren't dependable, it must mean that she was not lovable. Therefore she now internalized the profoundly wounding message, You're not worthy of our love. Actually, her parents loved her a great deal. Still, this is how Paula interpreted the message, leading her to the next conclusion, Therefore you're not worthy of anyone's love—including your own. She had constructed a syllogism that seemed perfectly logical: People who can't even be loved by their own parents are not lovable. My parents don't love me. Therefore I'm not lovable.

In reality Paula's reasoning was flawed, because it was based on two false premises: first, parents—especially those in high-stress families—are perhaps the *least* objective benchmark by which to measure our intrinsic worth. Second, Paula's parents did love her—albeit in a very damaging way. So through the years she carried the burden of the faulty conclusion that had followed naturally from her false premises, enacting it irrationally as an adult with nearly catastrophic outcomes. Paula's lack of bonding in early childhood also made it difficult for her to bond in her adult relationships. The mistrust she learned as a result of her parents' unpredictability carried over into her primary relationship. Not only was she often unaware of what emotions she felt, but she was also unable to express her feelings openly--even when she could identify them. Revealing one's inner states calls for a trusting climate that, in turn, requires the ability to trust.

Unfinished business from the past doesn't simply disappear. If it is not dealt with, it remains buried inside. Then the wounded inner child resurfaces later in unexpected and troubling ways. When you don't recognize the source of your difficulties, you condemn yourself to repeat the same self-defeating patterns in your relationships, not knowing why you do what you do. You become stuck. A clue that you are repeating the old patterns that eventually let you down is when you begin to search anew, after the latest foundering relationship, for something or someone to fulfill your unmet needs. A part of you believes that if only the right person comes along, he or she will fill the gaping void within you—make up for all the love you've missed and, by reflection, make you whole by sharing with you his or her charm, wit, and wisdom. Paula did just that. The unacknowledged, unintegrated childlike part of herself that didn't want to grow up found a substitute for the father hunger she experienced: she found a man old enough to *be* her father, who encouraged her dependence but who—like her real father—would also let her down at unpredictable times. She unwittingly reproduced a pattern that had started before age two.

THE WOUNDED CHILD IN RELATIONSHIP

When the inner child is not integrated into your total being, it expresses itself in any number of indirect ways destructive to relationships. Not everyone, for example, becomes chemically dependent and forms a reaction against other dependencies (that is, becomes counterdependent), as Paula did. In fact, the opposite is often true. When women first start dealing with their relationship addictions, they often ask, "Why is it that I can be so competent in my work and centered and active in my personal life when I'm on my own, and then, the minute I meet that 'special' other, I become this wimpy, dependent female who can't move without taking her cues from him?"

When people "fall in love," they experience a temporary desire to merge with the object of their love—to "lose themselves" in the other. This is typical. At an unconscious level, falling in love is a universal wish to replicate the primary relationship of the newborn infant with the object of its love, its mother (or primary caregiver).

The problem occurs when the compelling, ecstatic quality of romantic love intensifies, when compelling becomes compulsive. Whereas people who are not relationship addicts move out of the in-love phase rather quickly, recognizing the experience for the fleeting fantasy that it is, relationship addicts strive for constant and endless merger, wanting to lose themselves in the other.

RELATIONSHIP ADDICTS AND PERSONAL BOUNDARIES

Loss of self is a boundary issue. As mentioned in Chapter 2, personal, or ego, boundaries are the point at which one person stops and the other begins—boundaries have different degrees of permeability. Healthy people and families have boundaries that are permeable enough to allow for empathy and intimacy *without loss of self.* By contrast, one characteristic of dysfunctional families is the lack of boundary differentiation among its members, which can show up as one of two apparently opposite polarities that are actually two sides of the same coin: enmeshment (intrusiveness, failure to recognize invividuality, narcissism, and so on) or emotional cutoff (lack of meaningful communication, emotional withdrawal, disengagement, and so on). For a child in such a home, the struggle is to develop a healthy sense of self—with boundaries neither too rigid nor too permeable—while maintaining a family connection.

When a relationship addict enters a new relationship, her boundaries may be weakened on two scores. First, she may have grown up in a dysfunctional family that prevented the development of strong ego boundaries. Second, the experience of falling in love is likely to have made whatever boundaries she had even more permeable. In the addictive process, she may lose her boundaries completely. She may lose her self.

The more the potential partner triggers the primary childhood relationship—through physical appearance, words, actions, or other nonverbal cues—the more likely a relationship addict is to get hooked. The other person at first maybe unaware of what is happening. As the relationship addict reenacts the early childhood drama, bending over backward to please and to perform, her partner starts to feel stifled and begins to back off.

Humans function differently at different levels of anxiety, and relationship addiction adds enormous anxiety to a person's life. When people are in addiction-free relationships (or free from addictive relationships), they can channel their energy into constructive, self-enhancing activities that help keep anxiety at a reasonably low level. By contrast, when people's dependencies have been triggered, both stress and anxiety increase. Their ability to control their emotions decreases—

they become controlled *by* their emotions and lose a sense of their true selves.

As Paula's story illustrates, when a relationship addict loses her sense of balance because of escalating stress and anxiety, her self-esteem is also affected. While showing an ever greater need for attention and reassurance, a part of Paula was humiliated at her own dependence. When her partner increased the distance between them, this became an irresistible challenge for her. Like anyone dependent on an addictive substance, the thought that she might lose what seemed like an irreplaceable source made Paula even more anxious. The only way she knew how to preserve her supply was to become more controlling and demanding.

Such tactics are bound to make things worse. First, the partner is likely to withdraw, in an attempt to avoid being swallowed up, feeling his or her personal space to be threated by the addicted partner's intrusiveness. Second, the relationship addict's focus on "we" and her insistence on greater closeness is likely to intensify the common "I" versus "we" struggle between autonomy and togetherness that applies to any relationship. If the relationship addict's partner grew up in a dysfunctional home, the demand for closeness may also trigger the emotional cutoff that is the other pole of lack of boundary differentiation—polarizing the two even further.

RELATIONSHIP ADDICTS AND SELF-ESTEEM

The sense of low self-worth triggered by the new relationship challenge typically causes the relationship addict to take one of two extreme positions, either staying fixed at one of these two poles or alternating between them. At one extreme, in reaction to her inner feelings of insecurity and low self-esteem, she may act the part of the self-righteous, innocent victim. In this case she is likely to place full blame on her partner, refusing to accept any responsibility for his or her distancing behavior. At the other extreme, convinced that her partner would treat her differently if only she were lovable enough, she may take complete responsibility for her partner's distancing. A central issue in her life has come full circle: she has recreated her childhood struggle to be loved by her parents, interpreting her inability to get what she needs as a lack in herself. She feels she must *earn* love.

Because of her belief that becoming more lovable is the answer, and because of her irrational fears of rejection and abandonment, the relationship addict may try to hide her own perceived inadequacies from her partner. As a result she may become defensive and afraid to acknowledge mistakes and feelings of vulnerability, disowning a part of herself.

This behavior becomes particularly destructive on several scores: first, denying aspects of herself separates the relationship addict even further from her inner core, her sense of self. Second, because she is unwilling to trust her partner with her true feelings, she creates a block to intimacy, which is the key to a healthy relationship. Third, self-love, and the understanding that love is not earned, are necessary conditions for self-healing. Only when she embraces and loves her wounded inner child can she free the child—and herself—from the age-old shame and responsibility it has been carrying for what may have been the parents' inability to love or to love well.

RELATIONSHIP ADDICTS AND DISOWNED FEELINGS

Sometimes relationship addiction triggers deeply buried early infancy rages like the one that Paula experienced as a two-year-old as she screamed and shook her crib bars to get the attention to which she felt entitled. The relationship addict begins to see the partner as an extension of herself—there only to meet her needs. When the partner refuses to comply, she may become outraged. In her state of mind, it is as if her right arm had suddenly refused to function. Needing an outlet, she will turn this destructive rage either against her partner or herself. Such narcissistic rages are typical and normal in infants and young children, but inappropriate for adults.

The young child looks to its caregivers to soothe it and to provide an accurate mirror of its feelings. The mother who responds with empathy when her child falls and hurts itself, for example, validates the child's emotional state. This allows the child to fully experience, and let go of, its feelings. But a child who grows up in a troubled family that does not readily supply mirroring buries its unmet needs and unexpressed emotions. This is one more way in which a child may experience a psychic wound that can resurface quite destructively in adulthood.

Another way in which feelings resurface later, especially those that were either too threatening or too frightening to be expressed by the child, is through projective identification, a process by which such disowned feelings are unknowingly assigned to the partner. In a kind of unconscious collusion, the partner may then act out or "carry" that feeling for both of them, allowing the person that repressed it to continue disowning it and to separate even further from it. Such was the case in Paula's primary relationship. Trying to fend off her growing inner dependence, she became ever more independent externally. In counterpoint, her partner came to be more and more dependent on his first family, something for which Paula—blind to her own dependencies—showed both disapproval and contempt. He acted out the dependency for both—yet Paula was the more dependent of the two.

Unless something intervenes to change the destructive dynamics of such relationships and the downward spiral of addiction, the relationship continues to deteriorate. Unlike healthier relationships, however, the failure does not necessarily result in an ending—a separation or

divorce. Because the partners are usually enmeshed in mutual dependencies, carried primarily by the identified relationship addict, the relationship failure may manifest as physical or emotional illness or, in the
worst case, even suicide.

RELATIONSHIP ADDICTION AND WOMEN

It is common knowledge that women are more likely than men to
become relationship addicts. This is no great surprise, given both the
importance of relationship to women and the effect of socialization on
them. Women traditionally have attached much greater significance and
higher priority to relationship than men, often willing to make all kinds
of sacrifices when the nurturance of an important emotional investment
is threatened. Although women's relationship values are an important
and crucial social resource, our society grants much lower status to relationship, emotional expression, nurturing, and vulnerability than it
does to rugged individualism, self-interest, toughness, measurable output, and strength expressed as power over others.

As a result, women's strengths have been seen as weaknesses. Men
have the technological, physical, and financial power in our society. Because of this power imbalance in male–female relationships and in society at large, the dynamics are those of any typical dominant–
subordinate arrangement—an analog for the dynamics of addictive relationships. By definition, dominants don't consider subordinates equals.
They rely on power, not negotiation, to get what they want. Subordinates, on the other hand, depend for survival on pleasing dominants;
therefore subordinates have to learn as much as possible about dominants in order to please them.[5] Women's dependence and subordination,
in other words, are reinforced as normal. Although this is not to imply
that a simple cause-and-effect connection exists between our social climate and women's proneness to relationship addiction, its importance
as a contributing factor cannot be dismissed.

FINDING YOUR TRUE SELF THROUGH YOUR INNER CHILD

Although we share our common humanity, each of us is unique. Like
fingerprints, each person's essence—the core self—has special qualities
that have never been, and will never be, duplicated. Each person therefore makes a special, unique contribution to the world and to the lives
that she or he touches. We are also resilient; despite setbacks and struggles, we are geared for survival. We carry within the potential and need
for healthy and creative growth. According to Carl Jung, we are always
on a search for wholeness and completion, yearning for rebirth.

In the addictive process the fears and scars we carry from our past
tend to hide our true, most vital core, or self. We see only its reflection,
a false self we experience as boring, incomplete, sometimes depressed.

We fix on something outside ourselves to change all this. But the initial euphoric phase of a love affair turns into increasing dependence, in a process that is filled with peaks and valleys of alternating pleasure and pain. Despite all this, how we experience ourself has not changed, because we have placed all our hopes on changing the environment instead of ourselves. A popular quip is that true insanity consists of doing the same thing over and over again, yet expecting things to turn out differently. The pain, dependence, and unpredictability subside only when we own our past and empower our true self to leave the forest of fantasy and to create a better present.

Paradoxically, it is only when we let go of external expectations and go within to reclaim our neglected inner child that we can deal more effectively with the outer world. *A fundamental touchstone in recovery from childhood scars and from extreme dependencies is surrender to the idea that we cannot control others.* We attempt to control out of old fears of the unknown. And yet it's a delusion to think we can control others. At best, most of the time we have control over ourselves. This letting go is a universal truth, and one that is a cornerstone of Twelve-Step groups.

One of the rewards of reclaiming the inner child is that in doing so we get in touch with the childlike part of ourselves—the part that is most natural, creative, playful, and innocent.

SOCIETY'S DEFINITION OF ADULTHOOD

In order to survive, children from dysfunctional families take on overly rigid roles—so rigid in fact, that they are practically like scripts, filled with parental injunctions and obligations the child internalized early on. Life at home was serious business; adults from such families have often lost the capacity for enjoyment, for play. As shown by Paula's superwoman approach to life, such people seldom allow room for balance—for play, for fun, for time spent aimlessly. Allowing expression to the inner child breathes life into the intense seriousness with which they tackle daily living and relationships.

Getting to know and appreciate your inner child allows you to reclaim those parts of yourself that society has denigrated and disavowed. Our society values being an adult and "acting like an adult." And acting like an adult means being serious, no-nonsense, productive. Based on a mentality of "time is money," idleness is suspect and success is measured by tangible output that yields a monetary value in the marketplace. Thus, middle-class values create more injunctions and obligations.

In many ways this model of adulthood supports and echoes the unhealthy climate of a dysfunctional home. As in the dysfunctional family, it is based on a deprivation model, feeding into fears of not getting enough, not doing enough, not being enough. As a result it glorifies hard work—which explains why workaholism, an addiction, has received so little bad press. Being overtly childlike would be totally inappropriate at work. As in the dysfunctional home, there is an attempt to control others by withholding approval: someone who does not conform to the accepted idea of adulthood is looked on as suspect.

Because of the social stigma attached to "nonproductive" play, play surfaces in various disguises that are somewhat more acceptable. But disguised play works primarily for men, who can replicate into adulthood their competitive and adversarial win/lose childhood games through participation and spectatorship in team sports or by becoming vicariously involved in politicians' sabre rattling; and they can attempt to fulfill their recognition and power needs by driving flashy, powerful wheels. Boys' play is oriented toward individual, competitive activity and performance.

Little girls' play is very different. They are socialized to play with dolls, to play dress up, and to play house. Girls' play, in other words, is training for their traditional female adult roles. Girls' play is often based on cooperation. Girls also tend to play in smaller, more intimate groups than boys do, often just with a best friend, and in private places.[6] As a result of these differences in their way of being in the world, boys' *play* leads to men's *play,* while girls' *play* leads to women's *work.*

REPARENTING THE INNER CHILD

Finding and reparenting the inner child is predicated on full acceptance of yourself. Here again, our culture has made growth into wholeness particularly difficult for women. The fairly typical struggle of a therapy client who was just beginning to reframe her childhood experience provides a poignant illustration. At first this middle-aged woman was very impatient and derogatory when describing herself as a little girl going off on her first day of school. She referred to herself as an "obnoxious little kid," denying the child's right to express its need for nurturance and support. It was as if her self-condemning comments had come directly from her critical and punishing father. By accepting his view she had not only rejected the child in herself, she had also split off the feelings of this child. When, one day, she was finally able to actually reexperience the feelings of loneliness, fear, and uncertainty the little girl had felt, she burst into tears of sorrow at having for so long supplied nurturance to others in her life, all the while denying the same tender compassion for herself. She noted, "I care for others sometimes like a sheepherder. I watch and notice and pay attention to their distress. It isn't that I'm just totally accepting because sometimes I point out if I think they're off the mark or something, but I put myself in their place and I understand. With myself, though, I used to be like a lion tamer with a bull whip."[7]

Society's negative messages concerning women's emotionality and their expression of "selfish" needs feed into the tendency of women to take care of others at the expense of themselves. As a result, as the client's comment expresses so well, women have ministered to others' needs much more than they have to their own, at times becoming so sensitive to the distress of others that they have ceased to act in their own best interests.

As women, we have refined one aspect of empathy to an art—the capacity to enter someone else's subjective world and share the other's experience from that place with openness and nonjudgment. In reparenting ourselves now we need to develop the other crucial aspect of empathy—the capacity not to lose ourselves when entering someone else's boundaries. This is the key to healthy relationships. In addition, we also need to develop self-empathy, the ability to be compassionate and empathic with ourselves.[8] We need to transfer our ability to empathize to our own inner child, in other words, we need to look at and feel for our own inner child as we would for another human being. Maybe then we will be able to nurture ourselves. This, however, is a difficult task in a social climate that devalues women.

DEVELOPING THE SELF

A major reason why women's experience and roles are not fully appreciated is that traditionally child development theorists have written about "children"—encompassing both genders as if their experiences were completely alike. In addition, most traditional child development theories have been elaborated upon and filtered through a male experience. "Woman" is usually footnoted as having been included under the generic "man."

Current developmental assumptions are based on a separation–individuation model, which implies that people go through a number of stages of separation in order to form a distinct sense of self or personhood. Developmental theory, in other words, stresses the importance of separation from the mother in early stages of childhood development, from the family in adolescence, and from teachers and mentors in adulthood in order for the individual to form a distinct, separate identity.

Interestingly, the most popular and widely accepted of such theories—the eight stages described by noted psychiatrist Erik Erikson—places high value on the child's development of autonomy, self-reliance, independence, self-actualization, and on following one's own destiny. Then, in adulthood, the person is expected to move into intimacy and generativity: this, after years of separation and individuation, which are the very opposite of intimate relating. In other words, according to traditional developmental theory, people are to develop intimacy without ever having practiced it! By contrast, new theories that focus on women's experience suggest that for women, development takes a different path, which is not interrupted but continuous, and which is *relational* from infancy onward. The new theories challenge the traditional developmental model as inaccurate and incomplete for *both* men and women, but—because of societal influences—particularly so for women.

For example, in the first of Erikson's eight stages of life, the stage that spans the first year, the central goal is the infant's development of a sense of basic trust. But another important dimension is that the infant—and this is encouraged much more if it's a girl—begins to act like and be like the main caregiver, usually a woman. Rather than identifying with a static figure, the infant starts to develop a sense of itself as a "being-in-relationship." This is the start of a sense of self that reflects what happens *between* people.[9] In Paula's case, little actually happened *to* her as an infant. Her sense of failure stemmed from that first failed relationship—from what did *not* happen *for* her interpersonally.

Erikson identifies autonomy—which others have called separation and individuation—as the goal of the second stage of childhood (ages two to three). The new theory suggests instead that this is a period when the child uses more mental and physical resources and develops an enlarged sense of how it sees things, including a new understanding of, and new configurations in, relationship. For little girls, autonomy expresses itself not merely as a "doing," but rather as a "doing *for*"—for the mother and for others. She takes her cue from what Mother is still doing with little children: attending to their feelings and doing things for them. By this age little boys are taking their cues more from their fathers than their mothers. So action has a specific character; it takes place in relationship. The little girl uses her increased powers and opinions about how and what she wants to do. Rather than needing separation, maintaining relationships with the important people in her life is the most important thing.

The third stage, whose goal is initiative, is described by Erikson as one in which the four- and five-year-old child develops a sense of purpose and expanding mastery. Girls by this time, however, are receiving society's insistent message that they are to start focusing their natural attunement to others on the well-being, growth, and development of men. Depending on the social and ethnic background of the family, even the mother herself may encourage and model this way of being, encouraging the girl's turn toward the father. Despite its complexities, the girl's strong relationship and connection with her mother and other females continues. Yet the ascendancy, value, and power of the father are underscored while, psychologically, the mother is devalued. Recall the client who referred to herself as an "obnoxious little girl" because at first she could not see herself other than through the derogatory, unloving filter of her father's criticism.

Erikson identifies the fourth stage, between ages six and eleven, as having industry as its goal. Supposedly children are in a state of latency—when sexuality is on hold. Yet when it comes to relationships, girls are very active during this period, especially in their relationships with other girls. They often also show an active interest in boys and men, but boys are either not interested in them or are openly contemptuous of them. Girls at this age often sit together "just talking," much of the time about relationships in their lives. For different reasons, both Paula and Marcia at this age were isolated and alone, missing the chance to practice healthy relating with their best friends. Paula, without siblings, and separated from her parents by her rage and their alcoholism, buried herself in her studies, spending much of her time poring over books in the library. Marcia, repeatedly uprooted, treated in an unloving way at home, and rejected at school, first sought the intimacy she yearned for through a series of early sexual encounters, and later, by condoning in her marriage the brutality that echoed her childhood experience.

In other words, women's experience is not one of individuation through separation, but one of differentiation through relationship. What the new model of development emphasizes is that the direction of growth is not toward the breaking of early emotional ties, but "toward a process of growth within relationship, where both or all people involved are encouraged and challenged to maintain connection and to foster, adapt and change with the growth of the other."[10]

As mentioned earlier, although this model of a "self-in-relationship" is profoundly validating for women, it can also create for them the dangers of fostering the growth of others at the expense of self. The "woman on a pedestal," whose praises have been sung since before Beatrice led Dante into heaven, is not merely a romantic fiction created by men. Based on women's way of being in the world, it is an expectation imposed on them by men.

To give just one of many current examples of the penchant of women for becoming midwives to men's higher selves at the expense of their own, we can look at a study done in the preceding decade on the dynamics of men and women's support groups. A research team found that when women were placed in women-only groups, discussion focused on feelings, emotions, and personal experiences. In an eight-week period, the leadership role rotated among the group members. When men were placed in men-only groups, the leader emerged within the first two sessions and remained the dominant person throughout the eight-week period. In the men's groups discussion centered on activities, competition, and skills. When men and women were placed in mixed groups, the men became the leaders and dominated the session. Content also changed. The discussion became less competitive and focused less on activities and skills. There was also more discussion of feelings by the men. The women, however, discussed their feelings less often. Basically, the women became facilitators for the men. The investigators concluded that the mixed groups had benefited the men, but not the women.[11]

It is time for us as women to reframe our sense of interpersonal obligation. It is time for us to change our frame of reference from *responsibility* to *response/ability:* it is the difference between an impulse and a deliberate choice, between the *obligation to react* or *to take charge* and the *ability to respond.* Many of us learn to make this distinction as our children grow: at first, because they are totally dependent on us, we feel responsible *for* them. As they grow more and more self-sufficient, gradually we learn—sometimes from them—that what they need from us is the ability to respond. They no longer need us to respond *for* them; they value our willingness to respond *to* them.

But it's not children who are of concern here—it's our partners. For ages we have accepted responsibility *for* other adults, especially men, (while feeling accountable or responsible *to* society or to men for the discharge of that obligation). It is time for a shift, time to filter our responses through our own subjective experience. If we are to be responsible *to* anyone, let it be to ourselves first.

EXERCISES: FINDING YOUR INNER CHILD

The exercises that follow will help you to get in touch with different aspects of your childhood and to experience your inner child. Because their effect is cumulative, it is best for you to complete all four exercises in the sequence given, allowing some time between each.

EXERCISE I: SCRIPT INVENTORY

As children all of us internalized messages from our parents and ourselves that we have carried into adulthood, heeding them long after they have outworn their usefulness or the survival value they may have had at one time. Whether such messages were actually given, whether they were of our own making, or whether they were our distorted interpretations of reality, their long-range influence can be equally destructive.

As Alfred Adler and other psychologists discovered, some people may become so stuck in these childhood scripts that they can't live any part of their lives spontaneously or make decisions based on what is real. They make jet-age decisions using a Wright Brothers model. The good news is that once you detect that you may be living parts of your life based on an old script, you can reevaluate and change your behavior.[12]

1. What was your earliest favorite fairy tale, childhood story, TV story, or famous person?

2. With what person in the fairy tale or story did you most identify?

3. Do you see any metaphoric or symbolic parallels or connections between the emotional state of the character and your emotional state at the age when you liked the character? Do you see any metaphoric or symbolic parallels or connections between the emotional climate or situation described in the story and the emotional climate or situation of your family at the time?

4. Do you see any parallels between this character and your way of life (in terms of what the character does, how he or she does it, to whom or with whom, and what ultimately happens to him or her?) What are these parallels?

5. When you were young and your parents would talk about you, they would usually describe you as being. . . .

6. Your teachers usually thought of you as being. . . .

7. Currently your peers usually think of you as being. . . .

8. What do you wish people would say about you?

9. As a child you experienced a number of *major* "don'ts" from your parents or some significant close adult. In six words or fewer, complete the "don'ts" as you experienced them in childhood.

Don't. . . .

Don't. . . .

Don't. . . .

Don't. . . .

Don't. . . .

Don't. . . .

10. As a teenager you experienced a number of *major* "don'ts" from your parents or some significant other. Complete the following.

Don't. . . .

Don't. . . .

Don't. . . .

Don't. . . .

Don't. . . .

Don't. . . .

11. As an adult you currently experience a number of *major* "don'ts" from others. Complete the following.

Don't. . . .

Don't. . . .

Don't. . . .

Don't. . . .

Don't. . . .

Don't. . . .

12. As an adult you currently experience a number of *major* "don'ts" from yourself. Complete the following.

Don't. . . .

Don't. . . .

Don't. . . .

Don't. . . .

Don't. . . .

Don't. . . .

13. Complete the following sentences in a few words:

As a girl I had to. . . .
    I could. . . .
    I couldn't. . . .

As a woman I must. . . .
        I can. . . .
        I can't. . . .

As a "lady" I must. . . .
        I can. . . .
        I can't. . . .

14. Recall your father's style of giving you recognition or positive reinforcement. What did he say? How did he look? How did he sound? In what context or situations did he acknowledge you most? Least?

15. Recall your mother's style of giving you recognition or positive reinforcement. What did she say? How did she look? How did she sound? In what context or situations did she acknowledge you most? Least?

16. Did your father discount you? If so, how? (Give two or three specific examples.)

17. Did your mother discount you? If so, how? (Give two or three specific examples.)

18. For what aspect of what you do or who you are do you seem to be getting the *fewest* positive strokes now? (Stroking is any act that implies recognition of another's presence or existence.)

19. For what aspect of what you do or who you are do you seem to be getting the *most* positive strokes now?

20. Who are the five sources that you currently rely on most for positive strokes?

21. Are there any aspects of your life in which you have been getting negative strokes? If so, identify both the nature and the sources of the negative strokes.

22. What kind of positive strokes are easiest for you to give? Most difficult? To whom is it easiest to give such strokes? To whom is it hardest?

23. Have *you* given negative strokes in the past week? Month? To whom? How did it happen? (Identify details of the situation, dialogue, and so on, that led up to the negative strokes.)

When you have completed the script inventory, spend at least half an hour reviewing and elaborating connections between various sets of questions. They may help you reexperience aspects of childhood relationship patterns with your parents that are clues to scripts you still carry with you.

For instance, some people find that at some level they still believe their lives are like those of the hero or heroine in questions 1–4. Others realize that the fairy tale or story they liked best at a particular early age was a very close metaphor for their own family dynamics. A young woman who related to Beauty in "Beauty and the Beast" recognized that, as in the story, her mother was very much out of the picture—detached and cold. Her father, like Beauty's father, was another weak, unsuccessful businessperson whom she loved very much but with whom she was also very angry for failing to provide a better life for the family and for not standing up to his bitter, nagging wife.

You may also find parallels between areas in which you got few strokes from your father (question 14) and current ones you identify in question 18. Or, if your family was not great about providing positive strokes, you may find you're not great at providing positive strokes for yourself: did you include yourself in the five sources of positive strokes (question 20)? And what kind of strokes do *you* give? (questions 22 and 23). Are you unwittingly repeating the very patterns of stroking from which you're trying to break away?

EXERCISE II: MEDITATION

Find an old snapshot or portrait of yourself as a child, and place it in front of you. Close your eyes. Breathe deeply, clear your mind, and relax for a few moments. When you open your eyes, focus on the picture for several minutes. Try to absorb the presence and essence of that child into yourself. Then record your thoughts and feelings about her—preferably using paper and pencil. If you don't like to write, you may want to use a tape recorder instead.

As much as possible, use a stream-of-consciousness approach. In other words, don't try to write good prose or elegant sentences. Put down your thoughts as they come to you—phrases, sentence fragments, images, recurring themes or words, and so on—without forcing an organization on them. It is your impressions, the blending of thoughts and feelings, that will be of greatest value to you.

→ STOP READING NOW, AND DO THE EXERCISE
BEFORE CONTINUING ←

Debriefing

The intent of the exercise was for you to go beyond the child's physical appearance, asking yourself some of these questions: who is she? What do I know about her? How old is she? What is going on in her life at this time? What is she feeling as the picture is being taken? What is she feeling about the situation? About the person taking the picture (if you know who it was)? What is she feeling as she smiles (or doesn't smile) in that particular way? Does the picture scene accurately reflect her life at this time? Or is it a lie? What do I feel for this little girl I still carry inside me? Were you able to get in touch with your love and compassion for her?

EXERCISE III. YOUR INNER CORE

The uniqueness, the essence of who you are, can get buried in the hardship and serious business of growing up in a high-stress family. This is especially true of the playful, creative side of this essence, which is a part of the basic equipment with which everyone comes into the world. As a little girl Paula's inner core always shone through. She was gregarious, and even as a small child her powers of observation and sense of humor made her a natural storyteller. She was so finely tuned to other people that even before she was old enough to go to school, she knew she could always rely on this strength to make new friends— young or old, simple or sophisticated. She was also very artistic. Ballet, her form of self-expression, was a source of pleasure and of positive strokes from teachers, peers, parents, and relatives. Above all, she relied on this creative outlet to soothe herself when family stress increased. Whenever her parents would lapse into one of their drinking binges, she would quietly lock herself in her room and dance to the music of her record player for hours at a time, losing herself in the sounds and the activity. In growing up, in her single-minded pursuit of success and performance, she gradually lost contact with this creative aspect of her self. With it she also lost access to a key source of nurturance and self-renewal. Later she took up dancing again as part of her recovery program. It has become one of the weekly activities to which she looks forward most eagerly.

Think back to your own early childhood. What were *you* naturally good at? What specialty were you known for by your neighbors? Your friends? What did your grandparents boast about when they talked about you? What activities were so absorbing, so naturally enjoyable that you could lose yourself in them? What was it that, if all else had been stripped away, no one could take from you? Where is *your* dance today? What will it take to put it back into your life? In what guise?

EXERCISE IV. INTEGRATION

When you have completed all four exercises, you are likely to have a deeper understanding of yourself as a child—then and now. Take time to integrate your experiences, impressions, and feelings from the previous exercises. Record them in the way that is most comfortable for you—either by writing down or taping your impressions.

By reading this chapter and completing these exercises you have taken your first step on the path: you have increased your self-awareness about ways in which your past may be affecting your present interactions with others. In addition to those ways discussed in this chapter, one important way in which childhood experiences are connected to adult relationships is through the carryover of rigid roles. Dysfunctional roles are the subject of the next chapter, along with a discussion of how to overcome the influence of scripts and roles by reparenting yourself.

CHAPTER 4

Spellbound: Past Roles in the Present

Who you are today is the sum of your family heritage and all your experiences. Although the development and experiences of your early years are unquestionably of major importance, nevertheless developmental maturation is only one aspect of a child: the role or roles the child took on in its family of origin is the other. Roles come about because of the human need to be in relationship with others, starting with the families in which we grow up. If there were no need to interact with others and to define the boundaries and process of such interactions, there would be no need for roles. And because roles are so central to the child's growth as a social being in relationship, neither the understanding of a child's experience nor the understanding of what we do in adult relationships is complete without considering childhood roles.

In dysfunctional families the roles are typically quite rigid. This lack of flexibility is reinforced by other family members and, often, even by the person playing the role. Just as people who lack a clear sense of self sometimes seek a kind of vicarious identity from the facade of a uniform, so individuals in dysfunctional homes try to bolster their feelings of low self-esteem and confusion by hiding behind the symbolic "uniform" of a role, with its clearly defined and predictable behaviors. Especially in abusive homes, children also become self-effacing in an attempt to avoid punishment. So to make themselves invisible, they welcome the chance to hide behind the often safer facade of a role. The trouble with dysfunctional roles is twofold: first, because they are a response to *external* cues, they are not the child's freely chosen expression of its *internal* state. Second, reacting out of a role limits the kind of free range of expression that is available when a person responds to the unique features of a particular situation. Although roles often do have some negative long-term effects, it is also important to recognize that young children do not have choices and roles become an adaptive survival mechanism.

The primary function of the family unit is to meet growing children's needs. One of the characteristics that sets distressed families apart from healthy ones is their reversal of this mission. They expect the children to meet the needs of the family. This demand is communicated in many ways—some direct, many subtle and nonverbal. Nonetheless, children get the message. Even when they are not pressed to take on responsibilities inappropriate for their ages, or even to reverse roles with a parent, such children know they are expected to serve the family by reinforcing denial, shoring up its self-esteem, releasing the often unbearable stress, or creating diversions from the intensity of pain.

CHILDREN'S ROLES IN DYSFUNCTIONAL FAMILIES

Roles and birth order affect troubled family systems in ways that are more rigid and more pervasive than in healthy families. The function of roles becomes a twist on what the family unit is supposed to be all about: a place of safety, nurturance, and learning, as well as a matrix for the development of identity for its young. Dysfunctional roles come about when the child feels unloved and senses its safety is in jeopardy. The external cues to respond to the family's unspoken demands are an imperative that tells the child that in order to survive, it must meet expectations.

One of the most widely used and useful of the current models of dysfunctional family systems identifies four childhood roles.[1] Although looking at roles does oversimplify to some extent, and by no means claims to be a comprehensive understanding of family dynamics, it does clarify an important level of interaction among family members.

CHILDHOOD ROLES AND BIRTH ORDER

Children typically take on two roles: one dominant, the other auxiliary. The dominant role is the one that the child assumes most often, that seems to come most naturally, and that the family seems to reinforce most. The auxiliary role is the one the child falls back on when some kind of block develops to prevent or discourage the dominant role. Most commonly the switch comes about because of changes in the family—bringing about subtle or major role shifts in the entire system. Someone's dominant role may also be usurped by a sibling or be abandoned during times of especially high or low family stress. Frequently the kind of dominant family role a child takes on has some connection to his or her birth order. Depending on the birth order, certain generalizations can be made about people, regardless of the level of family function—that is, the age of a child with respect to his or her siblings has an effect on him or her even when the family is not dysfunctional.

THE HERO

In a family with four siblings, for example, the oldest child has all the privileges of an only child for a while. But when the next sibling comes along, the oldest becomes a kind of dethroned monarch. At first it is common for this child to show regressive behavior. Eventually, in order to win back the parents' attention and approval, it starts to cope by identifying with the parents' values and rules. This identification process is also partly due to the fact that, unlike younger siblings, the oldest is born into an adult system, with only adults as role models. As a result of these dynamics, the oldest child often becomes the responsible one and the more conventional or orthodox among the sibling subsystem— a kind of family hero.

These role characteristics become rigid and more pronounced when the family is dysfunctional. This hero is overly responsible, rigid, perfectionistic, aggressive, and self-righteous. Because of this child's strong need to have its way and be in control, this child also often learns to use charm to its advantage.

THE SCAPEGOAT

In well-functioning families, second children tend to be more relaxed than the oldest. Such children are not particularly concerned with being the center of attention, nor are they as sensitive to territorial encroachment. Their skills at negotiation and compromise are more finely honed than those of the oldest.

In a dysfunctional family the scapegoat is the child most responsive to peer values and peer pressure, acting out (truancies, pregnancies, shoplifting, chemical usage), withdrawing, and acting sullen and disengaged at home. The excitement caused when it misbehaves is self-reinforcing. By their own admission, scapegoats sometimes deliberately set out to cause trouble just to escape boredom.

THE LOST CHILD

The third child in a low-stress family often gets a great deal of love and attention. Because it wants to do what its older siblings do well, the youngest of three frequently develops a strong sense of competition. When it discovers that it cannot match the older siblings, this child usually learns to compensate by excelling at something uniquely its own. When there are only two children in a family, this competitive spirit is often taken over by the second child—especially if the two are of the same sex.

By taking on the role of the lost child, the third-born in a high-stress family welcomes the chance to fade into the background. This is especially common if a fourth child is born to a family, because then the third child loses its privileged youngest position—like the oldest child's dethronement. Unlike the oldest child, however, the third of four does not have the option of being the hero, a position that is already taken. It becomes the shy, quiet, timid, and aloof child who distances itself from others by retreating into its own private world of fantasy to avoid conflict and emotional pain, becoming lost to itself and the family.

THE MASCOT

In functional families the fourth or last child is often the most relaxed and cheerful—the one who laughs most readily. This may be partly because the parents have relaxed their child-rearing practices by the time a fourth child is born, and partly also because of playful and loving interaction with older siblings.

In troubled homes, on the other hand, each child that comes along finds it more difficult to get the parents' attention, because there are so many children and several roles are already taken. So the fourth child commonly creates the role of the family mascot for itself, and will do anything to attract attention. This child may entertain everyone with its great sense of humor, or with its cuteness and charm. Or it may distract the family with hyperactive antics.

FAMILY ROLE DYNAMICS

Looking at families as systems and at roles within the system as slots or ecological niches that need to be filled, we can see that when one role is filled, fewer options are available for the next child who comes along. But role realignments continue to take place when shifts in a family occur; they are designed to reestablish balance to the system. Such realignments also give children an opportunity to move into different positions—moving from a primary, or dominant, role into a secondary, or auxiliary, one, for example.

Recall Nate and Sarah, the two siblings described in Chapter 2. Nate, the older of the two, had taken on the dominant role of hero after Sarah's birth. Later a shift in the delicate equilibrium of the family system was brought about when Sarah became a junior golf champion, compensating for her inability to compete on Nate's academic territory. Suddenly the hero's position was being challenged. Nate, the family's high performer in academic subjects and extracurricular school activities, had always been the undisputed holder of that family role. Now he was no longer the only one to bring home trophies and awards. Sarah, the younger sibling and Nate's dethroner, was not only getting the attention typically lavished on a younger child, she was threatening one of Nate's major strategies for getting special attention from the family: excellence. Nate, reexperiencing the trauma and pain of the original displacement from only child to firstborn, after a short time gave up the unspoken tug-of-war. For a time he abdicated the hero role to the usurper, retreating into the private, isolated world of the lost child, his auxiliary role.

BIRTH ORDER DYNAMICS

Birth order generalizations, like all generalizations, may need to be modified depending on special family conditions, changes that occur in the family, and the separation in age of the siblings. For example, birth order generalizations are invalid when one sibling is separated by more than six or seven years from the others. When the separation in age is this significant, it's like starting a new family. The lastborn tends to blend the characteristics of the youngest child of the second set with those of an only child. Only children are usually articulate, not as comfortable with sharing as children with siblings are, and more easily frustrated when their expectations are not met.

Finally, women's socialization may be another significant factor in exceptions to birth order generalizations. Because our society has devalued women, it is often difficult for firstborn girls to become family heroes. In many families positive reinforcement for the firstborn's approved behavior is reserved for boys—just as their achievements are more valued. Often the hero role is granted to the oldest girl only if the secondborn is another girl.

If the secondborn is a boy, then it is he who is most likely to be treated like the hero. This difference in gender treatment becomes more serious when life choices are made in families with limited incomes or narrow thinking. When the time comes to decide about college, the "firstborn's privilege" may be challenged if the oldest is female and the secondborn is male. In that case some families are willing to offer encouragement and financial support to a son, while discounting a firstborn daughter's interest in pursuing an education.

TINA

Tina's case illustrates one woman's experience growing up in a family that was atypical with respect to birth order expectations. Tina is the youngest of three daughters of a working-class midwestern family. She was born when her oldest sister was eighteen and her second sister fifteen. Tina's father, a lover of the rugged outdoors, had dreamed of having a son to share his interests. After Tina's birth he simply displaced his unmet expectations onto his youngest daughter, socializing her to be the son he couldn't have. As soon as she was old enough, he taught Tina to fly-cast, pitch a tent, portage and paddle a canoe, and clean, load, and shoot a hunting rifle. She became his constant companion on his weekend outings into the wilderness.

In terms of birth order, the fifteen-year separation from the nearest sibling meant that Tina was a combination only child/youngest child.

Ordinarily competition from her older siblings would not have been an issue. But the attention her father lavished on her, coupled with his treatment of her as a privileged son, caused her sisters to become extremely jealous of her and very angry at their father. To make things worse, he had been actively alcoholic when the two older daughters were young. They had experienced the desolation and pain of having a chemically dependent parent whose only love object was the bottle. By the time Tina was born he was in recovery, and the older siblings resented that the youngest was reaping all the benefits of his sobriety. As a result Tina's sisters formed the kind of two-against-one coalition we're familiar with from the archetype of the wicked sisters (or stepsisters) prominent in fairy tales such as "Cinderella" and "Beauty and the Beast"—as well as in Shakespeare's King Lear. This alliance continued even into Tina's adulthood. To this day she grieves her sisters' unbridgeable rejection and the denial of sisterly closeness.

WOUNDED FAMILIES, WOUNDED CHILDREN

In dysfunctional families roles fill an overall need for both the family and the child. As suggested earlier, for the child they provide a kind of defense system, a protective shield behind which to hide its vulnerability. Likewise, roles help children of addiction to meet their basic needs for attention. Regardless of the type of attention the role elicits, according to stroke economy theory it has more value than getting no attention at all—witness the sustained negative attention that the scapegoat receives and often seeks. No matter what role they take on, children in dysfunctional families fundamentally believe they do not deserve unconditional love and, each in their own way, try to get love or at least attention by playing their roles to an extreme.

HOW THE FAMILY DEPENDS ON ROLES

Individual childhood roles also fill certain specific needs for the family. *Family heroes* help the family's sagging self-esteem. With their compulsive need for perfection, typical heroes rake in award after award, school honors, and trophies for the family to show off. These accomplishments also give heroes a chance to prove their lovability, an important side benefit, given that they believe they must always perform according to the parents' standards of excellence in order to get approval, attention, and love.

Because heroes are usually oldest children, it is also not uncommon for them to become "parentified," taking on the role of the dysfunctional parent—becoming "adult children." Such children may not seek accomplishments away from home, but use the family arena as the single source of their powerful need for approval and control.

Scapegoats meet the needs of the family by being the unacknowledged carriers of the entire family system's dysfunction, in a process reminiscent of projective identification, although its mechanism is different. Like the unconscious collusion between partners in which one carries the feelings and acts out the dysfunctional behavior for himself or herself as well as for the partner who disowns it, so the scapegoat carries and acts out the family's pain and the dysfunctional interactions, anxiety, and stress of all the members. When the scapegoat gets into trouble for the *n*th time for disruptive behavior in class, for being caught one more time smoking pot in the gym's locker room, or for shoplifting, the family can relieve its high anxiety by focusing its energy on resolving the new crisis and by blaming all its problems on this child. The scapegoat accepts this poor bargain and the guilt; at some level he or she is willing to pay the price for a little attention, albeit negative.

The *lost child* supports the family by fading into the woodwork and by asking for very little attention from the beleaguered, stress-ridden parents. Like its siblings, this child believes it is unloved, unlovable, and undeserving of love.

Acting on this belief, the lost child time after time preempts the pain of this harsh truth by removing itself from the family's unnurturing reality and creating a world of fantasy with its own subjective reality. This child is content with the few strokes she or he receives from the grateful parents—"Mary is such a good little girl; she never makes any trouble!"

Most of the time distressed families are under a heavy emotional cloud. The home climate is one of gloom and doom, alternating with periods of brittleness when the children, hoping to make themselves invisible, gingerly tiptoe around the drunken mother on yet another rampage or the father suffering through yet another bout of depression. This is where the mascot comes in.

More often than not, *mascots* are family clowns—although at times they may be hyperactive rather than entertaining. The clown brings to the family a welcome breath of lightheartedness and laughter, releasing the pent-up tensions that no one else seems to know how to dissipate. The child's hyperactive antics provide a diversion from the family's problems.

Mascots' behavior is also self-reinforcing. By creating even a temporary shift in the heavy home atmosphere, they ease their own tension. The family's laughter or scolding provides additional strokes for both the clowning and the hyperactive behavior.

Even so, the mascot's lightheartedness can be misleading. The charm, the wit, the humor are not reflections of a strong, healthy inner self. To the contrary. In none of the four roles, including the mascot, does the behavior match the emotions; it is a reaction to inner feelings of low self-esteem.

Family Roles

The Family Hero

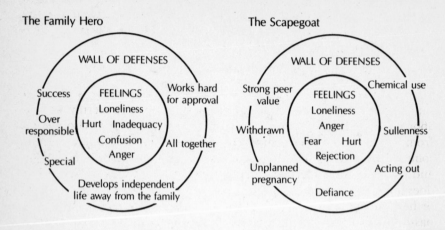

The Scapegoat

The Lost Child

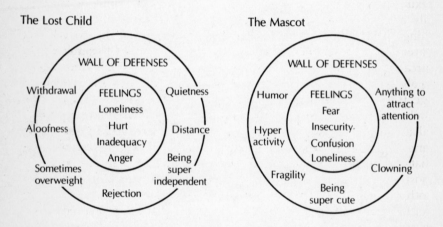

The Mascot

Figure 7

Source: "The Family Trap to Family Freedom," by Sharon Wegscheider-Cruse (*Alcoholism and Addiction* magazine, January/February 1985).

In fact, as shown in figure 7, these children typically build a wall of defenses in order to survive the feelings of hurt, anger, loneliness, guilt, fear, and sense of inadequacy that rage inside them. Having received little modeling for trust, they protect themselves against harm from others by hiding their vulnerability behind the shield of a role. The wall works both ways—it also creates a block to their ability to express emotions.

In time the disuse of this capacity to identify and then communicate their feelings—either to the conscious part of themselves or to some close relative or friend—dulls their ability to make fine discriminations. There comes a point when such children are not only unable to identify or express what is happening in their inner worlds, they become numb to their emotions, unable to feel at all.

THE ULTIMATE BETRAYAL

Of all the wounds a child may experience, family abuse is the most numbing and shattering. As children most of us were sternly warned about strangers and given strict instructions on how to protect ourselves from them. In reality most children are abused not by strangers, but by someone close to them—often someone in their own family. Satisfying and intimate adult relationships are predicated on trust. What effect does it have on a child when the person who is supposed to protect him or her, the one who says, "I love you," is also the abuser? Nothing surpasses the damage done by this double message, this profound betrayal.

Child abuse falls into three broad categories: emotional, physical, and sexual. By definition, growing up in a dysfunctional family is emotionally abusive. Emotional abuse occurs on a continuum, and includes things such as emotional unavailability on the part of the caretaker or parent, lack of validation, denial, mixed messages and double binds, sarcasm and other forms of derision, and so on. Children's vulnerability to abuse is affected by their role in the family and by their gender. To age twelve, boys and girls are at equal risk for physical abuse. After twelve, girls are at greater risk because older boys are more apt to retaliate, in part because of their greater physical strength. In our society girls are also at greater risk for sexual abuse. Statistics vary but most say that the overall risk for girls is four times greater than for boys. But most research agrees that sexual abuse figures are underrepresented for both genders, particularly for males. Social pressure is greater for men not to report sexual abuse. First, in a society that has promoted hypermasculinity, men are expected to like sex and to be tough. Second, because by far the greatest percentage of sexual abuse is perpetrated by men, males who were sexually abused are reluctant to speak up because of the stigma attached to homosexuality in our society, something that becomes doubly complicated and threatening when the abuser was their own father.

Overall, scapegoats and mascots are at greatest risk for physical abuse, because of their behavior. The parents may call the abuse punishment—either for acting out or for being hyperactive. Lost children are also at high risk for sexual abuse because they are often alone and isolated, don't talk to anyone, and get little attention. The other child at high risk for sexual abuse is the hero, especially when family circumstances place it in a situation in which its role and that of the mother are reversed.

The mother may be debilitated because of illness, too many pregnancies, or an addiction. Whatever the cause, the father often turns to the oldest child, especially if she is a girl, to take over the care of younger siblings and the household chores, acting as substitute mother. Sometimes he may also turn to her to meet his sexual needs.

Incest occurs on a continuum, from covert to overt. Overt incest is sexual contact, but the boundaries of covert incest are more blurred. Forms of covert incest include sexualized language and double entendres, "inadvertent" touch, reading lewd material to or in front of a child, or lack of privacy in bathroom or bedroom while bathing or dressing. One therapy client, for example, reported the rage she still felt in recalling her preteen years, when her father, under the guise of benign fatherly concern, would pull her close to him and cup her breasts, commenting with a leer, "Well, well, aren't we growing fast!"

A male client in his early thirties who had difficulties maintaining intimate relationships reported the strong emotional attachment that developed between himself and his mother after his parents' divorce, when he was a twelve-year-old "hero." It wasn't until years later—suddenly recognizing the seductiveness in his mother's voice, in her terms of endearment, and in the subtle ways in which she treated him like a special man—that he understood her expectation that he would fill her emotional needs, buying his loyalty through covert sexual innuendo.

As for overt incest, the research shows a ratio of 97:3 of father/child incest versus mother/child incest, but the experience of many clinicians indicates that mother/child incest is underrepresented. Nevertheless, even if that is so, the discrepancy is still great. One additional area of child sexual abuse that has recently become a focus of awareness is that of sexual involvement between siblings. As our understanding becomes greater, we are beginning to distinguish between normal sex play between children and instances in which a child abuses another.

Some significant differences exist in the ways men and women act out their emotional scars. The one exception seems to be children who were *physically* abused: unless there is an intervention, both physically abused men *and* women are likely to become physical abusers of children themselves. But overall, men who were abused as children tend to become abusers, while women abused as children tend to turn their anger on themselves or become enmeshed in relationships with people who abuse them again.

It is well documented that many rapists and incest perpetrators were victims of sexual abuse as children. And yet sexually abused women don't become rapists; however, they do tend to marry someone who sexually abuses their child. Or they may become self-abusive; they may starve, scratch, bite, cut, or otherwise mutilate themselves. Many women who are survivors of child abuse have eating disorders; some become prostitutes and/or addicts. Women's response to their childhood wounds comes out of their sense of powerlessness and learned helplessness. Men's comes out of their rage, which they then act out on innocent victims. Rape and incest are not sex crimes; they are crimes of violence. They are the ultimate boundary violation.

THE EFFECT OF CHILDHOOD ROLES IN ADULTHOOD

Dysfunctional childhood roles tend to follow people into adulthood, because they are self-reinforcing on at least two different levels. First, they were effective in childhood as survival techniques; second, they have become a familiar way to interact in the world. Unless a crisis occurs or a situation is reframed—that is, the situation is suddenly seen from a radically new point of view—most of us tend to avoid change. We choose to live in familiar ways that work poorly, rather than to risk the anxiety of the unknown. This is particularly true of adult children from dysfunctional homes. As a result of their often chaotic childhood home life, their great need for predictability and structure can easily become another form of rigidity. Unless there is an intervention, they are usually unable to stay aligned with the natural and inevitable flux of life's rhythms and events.

LIMITATIONS OF CHILDHOOD ROLES

The limitations of dysfunctional childhood roles become apparent in the adult interpersonal relationships of people who cling to those roles. As adults, for example, heroes find it difficult to be followers. When serving on committees, they may be poor team players. They might be disruptive or uncooperative, unless they are the ones calling the shots. Even then, because of the great need of heroes to control, their style may be perceived by others in the group as high-handed and arbitrary. Scapegoats, used to being in constant trouble as youngsters, may continue to create what they are most familiar with—excitement and chaos— in their personal and work environments. They may have difficulty keeping jobs, friends, or partners, blaming circumstances and others for their disappointments. Restless and easily bored, they may live on the edge, creating self-defeating situations filled with risks and dangers. Adult lost children, so used to being on the sidelines and to retreating quietly into their own private worlds, may find their career options dramatically curtailed because of their inability to speak out or advocate. The limitations may show up in a variety of arenas. One lost child may feel too exposed to successfully fill a PTA presidency, another may give up the dream of becoming an attorney, a third may find it impossible to perform in a commission sales job. Mascots, used to cracking jokes as children to get positive strokes—or to escape negative ones—continue to act the clown in adulthood. This is the only way they know how to make themselves liked. But when they want to be taken seriously, it may come as a painful shock to realize that the people around them can't see past the image of the happy-go-lucky joker.

At forty, Suzanne is a hero who is still stuck in her childhood role. As "supermom" to three children, ages twelve, fourteen, and seventeen, she runs the show for them and her husband. She runs herself ragged doing for them what they could be doing for themselves. As a result everyone in the family is deeply angry and resentful. Suzanne complains of feeling tired, exploited, and taken for granted—yet she is unwilling to surrender control. Her husband and children feel guilt-ridden for being unable to show the gratitude expected of them. At a deeper level they dimly understand that Suzanne's solicitous attentions serve primarily her own need to perform and to control by keeping others dependent on her.

Not only are rigid roles damaging to one's sense of self and one's ability to respond freely rather than to react, they are limiting, allowing for only a single, indiscriminate repertoire of behavior in all situations. In some ways the rigid role behavior prominent in dysfunctional families is reminiscent of the single-repertoire leadership styles many managers and executives used to have in business. Old-style managers, often acting more from their own negative belief system about employees in general than on the special demands of a situation or the people involved, did not question the wisdom of responding to every challenge in the same way. It wasn't until management theorists developed a *situational* leadership model that management practices changed to the more effective, efficient, and people-oriented approach now used in most U.S. corporations.[2] The situational leadership model points out that managers can't afford the luxury of responding with an often inflexible, single-repertoire style that "comes naturally." Instead the management style most appropriate to a situation must be based on an acute sensitivity to the people involved and on active listening, observation, and assessment of what is required in that particular case, taking into account a variety of considerations, such as employee skills and experience, quality of the manager-employee relationship, time available, and so on. In other words, just as in a good business, so in a family system the appropriate response cannot come from playing a rigid role, but only from an ability and willingness to observe and interpret each situation without posturings or preconceptions.

BENEFITS OF CHILDHOOD ROLES

So far, the negative aspects of roles have been emphasized; it is equally important to acknowledge some of their positive aspects. The hero's compulsivity and need for control, if balanced, can be channeled effectively to become assets in planning, organizing, and directing. The scapegoat's energy, love of excitement, and devil-may-care attitude can be directed toward high-mobility and high-risk work that would not appeal to others. The lost child's rich fantasy life and ability to be alone can help with self-sufficiency and perhaps even the pursuit of a profession in writing or the arts. The mascot's ability to laugh at life is an invaluable and healing resource to tap when the going gets rough, especially if the mascot can also laugh at herself or himself.

The following list shows some of the more common potentially positive and negative residues of old childhood roles:

HERO

POSITIVE	NEGATIVE
independent	fears rejection
meets goals	avoids risk-taking
powerful and in control	perfectionist
focused, attentive	doesn't get personal needs met
generous with praise	low self-esteem
organized	immature "adult-child"
responsible	unable to play
successful	unable to label feelings
leadership qualities	feels inadequate, doubts self
high achiever	fears intimacy
survivor	inflexible
loyal	fears failure
motivates self and others	guilt-ridden
	procrastinates
	fears confrontation
	driven to produce
	unreasonably high expectations of others

SCAPEGOAT

POSITIVE	NEGATIVE
lots of friends	substance abuser
adapts easily	manipulative
leads exciting way of life	passive-aggressive
handles stress well	rationalizer
traveler	often on the hot seat
commands attention	lies, makes up alibis
fun loving	daredevil
	irresponsible
	lacks close connections

LOST CHILD

POSITIVE	NEGATIVE
creative, imaginative	lonely, isolated, withdrawn
well-developed skills	lacks social skills
hobbyist	feels invisible, excluded
well-read	can be obsessed with self
spiritually developed	low self-esteem, distorted self-image
resourceful	sad, depressed
enjoys solitude	mistrusts, blames others
can work independently, alone	has difficulty connecting with others
nonconformist	fears reality
good manual dexterity	fantasizes life away
good listener, observer	inactive, indecisive

MASCOT

POSITIVE	NEGATIVE
sense of humor	never taken seriously
charming	depends on charm
joyful	denies own feelings to maintain image
eases family tension; keeps the peace	dependent
playful, active	irresponsible
attracts attention	seeks attention
	blames, projects
	deflects attention from real problem

People may drift in and out of their childhood roles at different times, depending on the quality of their lives at particular points. For example, as a result of counseling or the use of self-help techniques, someone may be living a relatively role-free life. Then, as a result of the increased stress of a difficult relationship, the same person may revert to the "comfort" of a familiar albeit dysfunctional childhood role.

KATRINA AND JACK

This reverting to a childhood role happened to Katrina, a twenty-eight-year-old administrative assistant. Before meeting Jack she had successfully managed to step out of the negative aspects of the roles, scripts, and injunctions of her childhood. But she slipped back into the familiar contraction spiral of addiction when she fell in love; she became the pursuer and Jack the distancer. As a child Katrina had played the active, assertive role of the hero, and Jack's main role had been that of the lost child—a passive, retreating posture. Feeling more and more rejected as time passed, Katrina's self-esteem sank to the point that her usually excellent performance at work began to suffer. In her obsession with Jack, she had given up meditation and her other spiritual practices. Suddenly she was getting very few positive strokes in her outer world's two most important and previously successful spheres—work and interpersonal relations—while at the same time failing to draw support from her inner world.

Unaware of what was really happening, she gradually retreated into her old, familiar childhood role. First she tried to escape facing her confusion and emotional pain by throwing all her energy into her work. Predictably, because society praises and materially rewards workaholism, she began feeling better about herself. But after a time her improved work environment was no longer enough to offset the feelings of rejection and abandonment she felt with Jack. So, unconsciously seeking positive strokes, she reentered the arena in which she had performed so successfully as a child. She enrolled in an M.B.A. program, and for a while the As, the professors' encouragement, and her peers' admiration were enough. But because she was neglecting her most important source of sustenance, the inner journey of self-discovery and self-healing she had begun years earlier, these external strokes failed her too in the long run. Only after she resumed her inner work did her relationships in the outer world start improving.

LOVE RELATIONSHIPS AND ROLES

Your relationship with the special other in your life is both the clearest mirror in which your childhood role is reflected and also the laboratory in which you have the opportunity to watch your dysfunction resurface and, once you recognize it, to strip it of its power and of its damaging negative elements while retaining its positive, enhancing aspects.

In close, intimate relationships heroes may resurface as active, assertive, controlling, and often guilt-ridden adult children who take the role of leader as a "given." Scapegoats may manifest as rebellious, blaming, aggressive, outspoken, angry, and critical partners with a victim mentality ("The world is unfair"), who at the same time are passive, self-deprecating, and accident-prone. Lost children may resurface by retreating into worlds of fantasy and hero worship in which flesh-and-blood people are made to fit into preconceived stereotypes. Adults stuck in the lost child role may be immature, vulnerable, isolated, and childlike—usually feeling overwhelmed by life's demands. Finally, mascots may frustrate and anger their partners by being routinely late, by making a joke of everything, or by surrendering their power through abdicating responsibility for themselves. Because they may have no clear sense of what is important, they may find it difficult to discriminate among priorities. Often mascots vie with heroes to be the attention getters. But because of the sophomoric quality of their humor, they may not be taken seriously in relationships. To see how these roles might actually play themselves out in a "slice of relationship," let's see what is likely to happen when someone unconsciously plays out his or her role in bed.

A *hero* sets the stage. A hero is a planner, so if it's up to her or him even casual sexual encounters are not casually decided, spur-of-the-moment events. Rather, they are carefully orchestrated. Being results-oriented, the hero will show interest in what the partner likes—and will keep count. The hero also likes to be in control and perform well. She or he is the more likely of the two to be the initiator of sexual play, which will probably be both creative and technically accomplished, and be the one who wants to be "on top"!

With a *scapegoat* in charge, there is likely to be little foreplay. As a sexual partner, he or she may be brash, lack sensitivity, and care only about his or her own needs. He or she may also be emotionally out of touch, distant, and guarded. Living in constant turmoil as a scapegoat often does, this person may be seething inside, generating active sexual energy out of repressed anger, which in a man may also express itself through premature ejaculation. The scapegoat's nonconformism and life on the edge may also find expression through sadomasochistic practices.

In bed a *lost child* is likely to be passive as well as submissive. She or he may use fantasy to offset a certain lack of passion, which also makes the lost child an unlikely initiator in a sexual encounter. She or he may be fearful of sexual experimentation and express dissatisfaction nonverbally through body language, yet fail to ask for what he or she wants. The lost child romanticizes even casual sexual encounters, and may even have fallen in love by the next morning.

A *mascot* is usually a creative, lighthearted sexual playmate whose curiosity and uninhibited love of fun may sometimes lead to one-night stands as well as unusual sexual arrangements and experiments. Playful, active, tireless, and energetic, the mascot at times may use humor to cover up emotional distance or to avoid intimacy. As a result a mascot may find the transition from sexual play to committed partnership daunting.

Rigid roles are to vibrant, vital relationships as a TV dinner is to a carefully and creatively prepared gourmet dish. The essence of relationship is the wondrous attunement that can take place between two people willing to be present with one another in the moment, interacting and responding without scripts, without preconceptions, and without agendas. Carl Jung once noted that, as with chemical substances, if there is any connection at all when two human beings meet, each emerges transformed from the contact. If either of them is stuck in a role as they reach out to one another, the possibility of breaking through the wall of defenses and making contact is lost, and so is the potential for transformation.

REPARENTING

Perhaps the single most powerful and effective way to step safely out of rigid childhood roles and heal the wounds of the past is to begin reparenting yourself—becoming a "good-enough" parent to your inner child. Children don't need perfect parents—something that is impossible to achieve anyway. Parents are imperfect humans; they merely need to be good-enough parents, people who are there for their children most of the time with goodwill, support, understanding, warmth, and gentle caring.[3] Likewise, in reparenting yourself, you need to be a good-enough parent to the inner child who needs no less nurturance than a "real" one to resume its arrested development. One of the problems is that people who grew up in troubled families are not always sure what good or good-enough parenting actually is. The list of good-enough parenting traits on page 86 was developed by women in therapy groups for adult daughters of alcoholics. These positive parental characteristics may prompt you to identify areas in which you need to begin reparenting yourself.

If you take seriously the proposition that reparenting is an integral part of self-healing, two important steps become necessary. First, you must commit yourself to investing time and energy in reparenting, just as you would if you had just adopted a child. Supporting and nurturing the inner child needs to become a priority, just as every good-enough parent would make it.

Second, you need to be *attuned* to the needs of the child within, something that requires empathy (the ability to sense the inner child's subjective world from its own perspective). Yet attunement is more than empathy. It is the sum of all sensory and intuitive information you are able to collect at any one moment about the needs of the child, coupled with the intent to meet those needs. Beyond that, it is the harmony between your adult self and the wounded child within you. Attunement to your inner child can be a first step toward love.

DESIRABLE PARENTING TRAITS AND QUALITIES

Much of the time a good-enough parent:

- Is nurturing
- Is flexible
- Is understanding

- Is consistent

- Allows growth

- Acknowledges the child as a unique individual
- Provides the basics and a positive emotional atmosphere (protection, safety, security, food, shelter)

- Listens without judgment
- Is accepting
- Provides direction and age-appropriate guidance
- Knows how to let go (is not possessive)
- Establishes and maintains rituals
- Is an ally

- Is a role model; models wholeness, balance

Keywords for a good-enough parent include:

- Attention
- Involvement
- Guidance
- Communication
- Comfort
- Validation
- Flexibility
- Understanding
- Education
- Cooperation

- Touch
- Consistency
- Structure
- Positive reinforcement
- Confidence-building
- Age-appropriate expectations
- Love
- Coping skills
- Hopefulness
- Trust (opportunities to earn it)

A good-enough parent avoids making a child feel "not OK":

- has and enforces a reasonable number of procedures, rules
- much of the time is not "too busy" to pay attention to the child
- speaks with the child without anger or irritation much of the time

EXERCISES: LEARNING TO REPARENT

With the three activities that follow, you have an opportunity to become attuned to your inner child and to create a reparenting experience that uniquely suits both parts of you.

EXERCISE I: CHILD/ADULT ROLES

Examine your childhood roles and their relationship to or power over your current life by recalling specific incidents or events during your early and later childhood (ages six or seven and eleven or twelve). If you have difficulties recollecting them, perhaps you can use old photos and family stories to piece together clues as to what your old roles were.

What was your *dominant* childhood role?
What was your *auxiliary* role?
When and how did you use the dominant role? The auxiliary?
What was your birth order in the family?
How did it detract from or contribute to your childhood experience?
In what ways do you still use one or both of your childhood roles in your life today?
How do they play themselves out with friends? At work? In personal relationships?

Roles have both negative and positive aspects. Analyze a current role behavior that reflects your dominant role when you were a child. How, specifically, does this role express itself in your adult life? What are its positive and negative payoffs today?

EXERCISE II: GOOD-ENOUGH PARENTING LIST

What is good-enough parenting to you? On the preceding list (include your own additions), mark those qualities which you feel were missing or present to an inadequate degree in the parenting you received. Then choose one and begin reparenting yourself in that area. For example, if you were a child who needed more affectionate physical touch than you received, you might consider treating yourself to regularly scheduled bodywork sessions. If you were an adult child, who had to take on an inordinate and age-inappropriate amount of responsibility for other family members, you probably feel guilty when you play or have even forgotten how to do so. Learn to fly a kite, go folk dancing, let yourself go and ride a merry-go-round—or buy that oversized helium balloon you always wanted when you were little!

EXERCISE III: YOUR ELUSIVE INNER CHILD

From the exercises done so far, and from relating the reading to your life, perhaps even from dreams, do you have a sense of how your disowned inner child gets your attention today? Think back over the past month: find examples of times when your behavior was childlike, or reactive like a child's, or frightened, overly sensitive, and insecure—unlike the way you usually are today.

For each behavior identified, describe an action you might have taken to reparent the child, instead of dismissing it gruffly or allowing it to go on an uncontrolled rampage. Usually the small child inside is overcome by fears, insecurity, or anger. First steps on the reparenting path include being empathic, understanding, and gentle—validating the child's feelings and addressing them openly. After all, that's what a kind parent would do with a child. Some people find it useful to carry on an actual dialogue between the adult side and the inner child, listening carefully to what the child says, and then moving to calmly reassure it and soothe it, ready to also set reasonable limits when the situation requires it. Others may feel comfortable reaching out to a close friend or partner with whom to be open and vulnerable, to allow this inner child to be held, loved, and nurtured by a trusted, intimate other.

EXERCISE IV: ATTUNEMENT TO YOUR INNER CHILD

Recall the exercises in Chapter 3. With the insights you gained from them and from Exercise III in this chapter, do you get a sense for your child's age? Feelings? Usual state of mind? Needs? Wants? List all clues you have about your inner child. Then devise a reparenting plan that suits its age and its needs. Remember these important bits of information when the child acts out. You can't treat a three-year-old the same way you would an eight-year-old. Even though the activities and exercises may seem uncomfortable or somewhat extreme at times, reparenting is a crucial aspect of self-healing that requires no less than complete commitment if you hope for intimacy in future relationships. Whenever you neglect your inner child, you expect someone else to take care of your needs. Neglecting your inner child interferes not only with your love relationships (Chapter 5), but also with your wider support system, such as friendships (Chapter 6).

Part II

THE PATH INTO THE LIGHT

CHAPTER 5

Steppingstones: The Building of Relationship

"The unexamined life is not worth living." If a single maxim could guide us as we begin to build healthier relationships, surely Socrates' dictum would hold the greatest promise. Part I of this book shed light on the power of the family and its effect on a child's experience. Now you can use the deeper self-understanding you have gained to help you examine the myriad ways in which your past is holding you captive in the present.

Understanding one's past is merely a first step, of course. The real work required to break the spell of the enchanted forest of self-deception and limitation is still ahead. Part II provides some of the tools and raw materials of relationship building you will need on this very personal journey. It is meant to help you question formerly unchallenged or unexamined assumptions you may hold about relationships. That they may have had their origins in dysfunctional modeling is not the only reason why long-held assumptions about love, commitment, and intimacy need to be reexamined. In this decade we are witnessing rapid and dramatic social changes and a shift in consciousness about how we can best relate to each other so that everyone gains, grows, and remains intact. Trying to meet contemporary relationship needs using our parents' and grandparents' yardstick is like trying to find one's way in a new city suburb with a thirty five-year old map.

THE LIFELONG PROCESS OF SELF-DEFINITION

Defining ourselves is a lifelong process that in a way resembles the proverbial peeling of the onion: whenever we reach a new understanding of our selfhood, we are likely to find that new aspects of our basic core issues are pressing just beneath our level of awareness, waiting to be uncovered, dealt with, and integrated into a self-understanding that is deeper still. This cycle goes on indefinitely. If we are receptive to it, it offers us again and again fresh perspectives of what life and relationships are all about. It is necessary to stay alert, to keep monitoring our sense of self, and heed our intuitions. It is important to observe and to witness, to avoid suppressing unpleasant facts and truths.

PARTNERSHIP

Whatever we have defined for and about ourselves, it is in the here and now of relationships that we undergo our continual testing and fine-tuning. Friendship may help us to clarify and practice our values, needs, and wants. But the true test of our introspective groundwork is in our love partnerships.

In partnership our boundaries, our motives, our definition of love are constantly challenged—along with our ability to communicate what we really mean. And yet, no matter how much we may know about communication techniques, our messages can be clear only if we ourselves are clear about who we are, what makes us tick. Computer people grasped this principle long ago. The acronym GIGO—"garbage in, garbage out"—may be unceremonious, but it makes its point.

Although communication ranks at the top of practically every study and opinion poll concerned with finding the common denominator of successful long-term love partnerships, obviously there is more to healthy love relationships than self-awareness and communication. Even though we may deny unpleasant truths to ourselves, at some level we usually know when we are not in a mutually supportive, satisfying love relationship.

Healthy long-term relationships have a zestful quality and vitality that reveals itself in the partners individually as well as in their interactions as a couple. There is a feeling of openness and connection between the two. Each seems to enhance the other's life in an expansive way that invites each to reach outside the relationship to explore her or his highest aspirations and potential. And, like a fingerprint, every successful relationship is unique. It is also true that there are certain qualities, attitudes, and skills crucial to a successful relationship. Just as in Chapter 2 we discussed ten key factors that identified healthy families, so in this chapter we will take a look at major steppingstones on the path to loving relationships: similarities, ability to deal with change, compatible values, effective and open communication, ability to resolve conflict and deal with anger, effective negotiation, firm personal boundaries, healthy sexual expression, shared quality time, and friendship.

SIMILARITIES

Introspection and communication skills are strong assets in relationships. Introspection helps us identify what we bring with us out of our dysfunctional childhood; skillful communication helps us express with clarity what we want or need.

Although similarities of temperament and shared interests between partners are certainly desirable, important, and fun, here we are addressing primarily core-level similarities of values and of needs and wants, some of which may be "frozen"—for example, unrealistic needs for attention or unconditional approval. Frozen needs are impossible to ever fill, because they are an unconscious way to hold onto unmet early childhood needs for love and attention from our parents. Not being anchored in the present, such frozen needs simply cannot be filled in the present—no matter how caring and giving a current partner might be. There may also be frozen fears: two of the most common are fears of abandonment and of engulfment. Still others may be emotions such as depression, grief, or feelings of rejection or exclusion that also carry over from the past into current relationships.

How well we are able to identify and acknowledge the frozen aspects of ourselves, and how well the legitimate current needs and wants we express match those of our partner, are indicators of a relationship's prospects. In Chapter 3 we spoke of projection and projective identification: if we project our unhealed and unacknowledged wounds from the past onto our partner, or allow him or her to do that to us, no true communication is possible, because at least one person is not dealing with current reality. Likewise, if we know that we are comfortable only in a committed traditional marriage, but our partner is most at ease in a fluid, open relationship, we can be sure we are heading for trouble.

In Gershwin's *Porgy and Bess,* both protagonists have been wounded by life. Porgy's body is crippled, but his real scars are emotional. Although beloved in his community, until he meets and falls in love with Bess, he is very lonely, without a special someone to share his life. When love blossoms between the two of them, Porgy wants very much for Bess to live with him on Catfish Row as his woman. Bess's attractive figure, full of vitality and swagger, is in stark contrast to Porgy's broken body. It belies her own inner turmoil, for she is herself deeply wounded by a chaotic past life she shared with Crown, a harsh and violent man. Even now, she and Porgy are still on very different paths.

For the first time in his life, Porgy glimpses the possibility of redemption of his wounded feelings through love, and although a part of Bess desperately wants to believe that this is possible for her too, it becomes clear that this won't happen on Catfish Row. Eventually she leaves, escaping once more into a world of drugs and glitter, still lacking the inner resources to counterbalance its allure.

Porgy and Bess were on an ineluctable collision course. Each of them sought salvation through something outside themselves—Porgy through Bess, and Bess through her senses—so the ultimate failure of their relationship was predictable. Although their love was real and powerful, it could neither bridge their fundamentally different ways of being in the world nor generate the spark of introspection that might have transformed them.

Because with your friends you are not likely to attempt to recreate your childhood relationships with your parents—as you may unconsciously do with your lover or your family—your friends, your lover, your spouse, and your children may experience you in very different ways. This may help to explain why friends are able to be so accepting. Over and over again clients in therapy speak with anger and confusion of their abusive parents, failing to understand how these could be the same individuals who were pillars of the community, beloved and respected by scores of friends and neighbors.

Even when you manage to bring into consciousness major childhood memories, it may take a long time to change the feelings they evoke. But at least you can begin to change your behavior and evaluate with greater clarity and fairness the expectations you have of your partner. One similarity to seek here is a partner equally willing to acknowledge and work on the dysfunctions he or she carries over into the present from childhood wounds. Another, even more important similarity, is a similarity of wants in a loving relationship. Ask yourself

> Do we agree on issues such as marriage, commitment, and monogamy—and in the way we look at relationship?
>
> Do we share similar views about the *meaning* of relationship in our lives?
>
> Is relationship an end in itself?
>
> Is it a setting in which to raise children?
>
> Is it an opportunity for personal growth?
>
> It is a chance to practice what we might do better in all our relationships?
>
> Is it a central enhancement and support of our inner lives and of ourselves as productive members of the community?

IF ONLY MY PARTNER WOULD CHANGE

Life is always changing, requiring us to change and adapt along with it. Because people do change, their needs and perspectives on life are also bound to change over time. In love relationships the changing needs of one of the partners can cause a major relationship conflict. Therefore the ability to deal effectively with change is a crucial skill in relationships. Like families, couples are minisystems that constantly strive to maintain equilibrium. Recall the analogy of the mobile in chapter two: when one piece of the mobile (or one partner) changes, it is inevitable that the other will also have to make adjustments to maintain or reestablish the system's balance. Almost invariably the immediate response is for the nonchanging partner to put a lot of energy into trying to get the person who is changing to change back—that is, to maintain the status quo.[1] If not, the nonchanging partner may have to make some adjustments—an often threatening idea.

Ironically, the change may have been prompted at the nonchanging partner's prodding. Growing up in a dysfunctional home, people may become blamers as adults, always holding someone else responsible for their unhappiness, an often successful ploy to shift the focus away from themselves. "If only she would spend less time on her work. . . ." "If only he would stop being distant. . . ." Blamers complain a lot, but they seldom think of the implications for themselves if the partner really does change. Their "if onlys" look at change as if it were a one-way street in which the only one needing to change is their partner. Yet from the systems model we know that no action occurs without a reaction. When you push for change, have you thought through what it would really be like if your partner actually did change? What if Jane really does stay home more? Are you prepared to give up some of your own free time? Perhaps make do with a lesser income? Cope with her dissatisfaction if her new job offers her less prestige? Deal with her sense of boredom and restlessness—or even with your own potential boredom if her life becomes less interesting? Can your own intimacy quotient handle it if George really does become less distant? If he wants to be with you wherever you go? If he sulks whenever you want to go somewhere without him? When you ask for change, you need to make sure that you don't set in motion forces you scarcely understand, and whose long-term implications you have failed to anticipate.

Because those in healthy relationships experience and acknowledge change, crisis and conflict are not uncommon—contrary to the myth with which some of us grew up. In fact, it is the relationship that claims no conflict or crisis which is suspect. Perhaps the partners are stuffing their feelings or the relationship is stagnant—whatever the reason, no significant changes are taking place within it.

Conflict is natural; difficulties arise when they are not handled with an open, win–win attitude—or when unconscious motivations come into play. It is equally true, however, that the greater the number of important areas on which the two partners are well matched, the less likely they are to experience frequent conflict. The notion that all relationships are hard and require a lot of work is another myth.

KNOWING AND SHARING YOUR VALUES

Some couples who come into therapy with troubled relationships never discussed or paid attention to each other's values when they met. This happens sometimes because they didn't realize this was important or didn't expect the relationship to become meaningful, sometimes because of the two individuals' lack of definition of their own value systems.

Usually common interests or passion (or both) drew such couples together. But you can't dance, sail, or gaze into each other's eyes twenty-four hours a day.

When a relationship moves into any kind of depth, values inevitably come into play. Political affiliation, stand on abortion, view on the peace movement, how, where, and when money is spent, way of life, religious practice—value issues are unavoidable. If a couple plans to have children, discussing values ahead of time is especially necessary, because otherwise value conflicts will surely become a source of much friction in parenting. Do the partners agree on parenting style? The sharing of parental responsibilities? The balancing of the mother's and father's work outside the home with the bearing and raising of the children? The religious upbringing of the children? The size family they want and can afford? Sometimes the real issue is disguised, and one kind of value may stand in for another, deeper one. For instance, someone's fiercely defended need for sexual freedom in relationship may disguise a more deeply felt need for general, unfettered self-determination, uniqueness, or individuality.

For all this, discussing values is not enough. It is not enough to be guided by what people say their values are, because a vast gulf may exist between what people believe they believe and what their actions and behaviors say about what they actually believe. A person's *real* values are reflected in how he or she lives, in what he or she does, rather than in what he or she says. Learning about people's values by observation takes time, and is an excellent reason for getting to know someone well before deciding which relationship is worth a long-term commitment. Unless in a love partnership there are strong similarities of values, or at least an ability to accept differences without harming your own core, the lack of agreement can become the source of deep-seated and perhaps unresolvable conflicts.

SAYING WHAT YOU *REALLY* MEAN

Good communication is fundamental to all human relationships. The clarity of intent behind the message is one key to being understood. Humans have a need to communicate. We need to share our thoughts, our hopes, our needs with those we care about, because it is primarily through communication that we connect with others. We cannot *not* communicate; even our silences tell their own stories, because communication takes place in different ways, not just with words. Studies show that words are only about 7 percent of the total message; 38 percent of the message is conveyed by qualities of the voice, and 55 percent by body movement.[2]

When a speaker is not aware of unconscious motives or clear about her or his intent when speaking, when words don't match body language or inner feelings, and when words or body language don't fit the context, then the result is a mixed message. The various levels of communication don't match. For clear and straightforward communication to occur, all levels have to be consistent—or congruent—with one another.

Most of us tend to focus on the content of a message when in fact, as illustrated by the ratios mentioned, communication is a *process*. In dealing with relationship issues, it is often more informative and productive to observe *how* two people communicate—that is, what goes on between them—than to listen to a blow-by-blow description of who is doing what.

Children who grew up in dysfunctional homes have had generally poor communication modeling. Denial, secrecy, unpredictability, inconsistency, anger, aggression, lack of self-awareness are all communication blocks—"noise." Past experiences and attitudes may create additional noise by coloring the messages that are received.

To make the challenge even greater, there is a discrepancy between how fast we can talk (an average of 125 words per minute) and how fast we can process what we hear (400 to 600 words per minute). What do most of us do during those 275- to 475-word intervals? We often jump ahead to prepare our response, which makes us lose track of what is happening or being said at that particular moment.[3] This, in turn, limits our response/ability by stereotyping the situation, as if it were an exact replica of some dialogue of the past.

Distressed families tend to blame and generalize. Their typical speech pattern is one of "You" messages. ("You always come home late for dinner without calling." "Now look what you've made me do!") These messages produce guilt and negatively affect young people's self-esteem. Above all, by placing the listener on the defensive, You messages cut off further functional communication.

"I" messages, on the other hand, merely state the speaker's feelings about a situation. Because such messages describe, they neither generalize nor attack the listener, thereby promoting open communication. ("I get worried when you're late." "I'm upset because your bed still isn't made.")

Good, clear communication can significantly reduce conflict by eliminating needless misunderstandings or buildup of resentments. But at times conflict is unavoidable, and learning effective ways of dealing with it is an important relationship skill. One of the most difficult and challenging aspects of skillful communication is to be able to integrate a sense of self-empowerment with a sense of compassion. This means being able to assert your feelings and needs while maintaining genuine caring and empathy for another.

RESOLVING CONFLICT AND ANGER

The closer the love relationship, the more individual differences become evident—and the greater the possibility of conflict. Yet individual differences are not necessarily a cause of conflict. Differences are not only to be expected, but they can be wonderful assets in a relationship, offering richness, vitality, and expansiveness. Individual differences may be one of the things that attracted two people to one another in the first place, and in many relationships differences are discussed up front, honored, and celebrated. Differences may also become challenges, especially among adult children of distressed homes, who typically lack some skills for dealing effectively with the conflict that differences may evoke. In their families of origin, conflict was probably rarely discussed openly or worked through in mutually acceptable ways. Agreement was seldom sought. Impasses were resolved either by allowing events to take over—that is, making decisions by indecision—or by unilateral parental edict.

Children from such homes learned little or nothing about *really* hearing everyone's side, about equity, about compromise. They particularly never learned about negotiation or about the concept of a quid pro quo (the more elegant Latin version of "You scratch my back and I'll scratch yours") that lie at the foundation of mutuality—the very opposite of unilateral, authority-oriented decision making.[4]

Dysfunctional families often deny anger; this denial is partly due to the fact that in such homes conflict is viewed as dangerous—and for good reason. When people with low self-esteem and with few communication and problem-solving skills try to deal with conflict, it is dangerous; the alternatives to reasoned discussion are escalation, flaring tempers, slammed doors, and family violence.

Anger is not necessarily negative, as long as it is clear—that is, as long as, despite its vehemence or intensity, it is confined essentially to an "I" statement that expresses an individual's feelings of frustration and it bears no threat of violence. On the other hand, anger is destructive when it is in any way out of control, when it creates a climate of violence, or when it attacks someone else either emotionally or physically. In intimate relationships anger is often a symptom of conflict that has been glossed over and a clue that something needs to be changed or dealt with. In dysfunctional relationships anger triggers lots of "You" statements and blaming—the other person is always the one who is wrong, who needs to change. In some relationships there may be much anger that is triggered by early childhood wounds. Until its source is uncovered and worked through, it can cause a couple to become discouraged and exhausted, feeling as though they are on an endless treadmill they only dimly understand.

Because of the effect unconscious motivations have on relationships, it is important to identify the primary cause of the conflict before making any attempts to deal with it. Is it an *interpersonal* issue, or is it primarily *internal* to one of the partners? Unless this identification or sorting-out stage precedes an attempted solution, even with the partners' best intentions the conflict is likely to go on.

RANDY AND JACKIE

Randy and Jackie both grew up in alcoholic homes. For two years they had been in a highly conflictual marriage that produced a lot of angry outbursts between them. Even though both cared a lot for each other and neither really wanted a divorce, they were starting to think it might be the only alternative possible, because nothing else seemed to work. They spent several sessions in couples counseling without making much progress. They could not seem to change the pattern of their interaction; their conflicts continued to be frequent, destructive, and exhausting. Then one day they brought in an "action script" of their most recent argument. Both worked in a video production house, and had thought of actually describing the incident as if it were a video program to be staged and filmed, so the therapist could visualize its details in her mind's eye. Here is a summary of the introductory section of their conflict script:

R (Randy) comes home and says hello rather stiffly. He is angry at Jackie (J), but doesn't want to get into yet another argument, so he tries to act normally.

J. knows him too well. She is not fooled. She feels a lot of anxiety about his being angry and wants to get it over with. She prods him about his coolness.

R. at first denies anything is wrong. Then, at J.'s insistence, and speaking quickly and intensely, he reminds J. of some very cruel things she had said to him the night before.

J. has suppressed the negative statements she made and remembers only several positive things she said. So she feels self-righteous and maligned. Simultaneously, she remembers some less-than-wonderful things R. said to her two days ago, and brings those up now.

R., neatly sidestepping the bait, readily acknowledges his shortcomings and apologizes, but now he is even angrier at J. He feels that her denial of her own verbal cruelty robs him of his experience and tells her so. He reminds J. of specific things she said.

J. feels a knot of anxiety in the pit of her stomach. Suddenly she remembers, and recognizes the legitimacy of R.'s complaint. Her old sense of inadequacy and insecurity is triggered and takes over. She is afraid R. will leave her, and experiences a wave of sorrow and discouragement, both at being so "bad" and at not knowing how to stop hurting the person about whom she cares the most. In deep frustration and helplessness, she gets up, picks up her purse, and starts to leave.

R., though, has picked up her keys and blocks the exit to the garage. He tells her to stay and talk things out. She struggles to get the keys and get past him. He insists she's not to leave. The original script goes on for several more pages. Eventually Jackie did stay, Randy and she talked things out, and for the first time something did change: they both agreed to sit down and document step by step what actions they each had taken, what was happening emotionally for them, and what meaning they each attached to the events as they were unfolding.

In recreating the events of that night, Jackie recognized for the first time that whenever she felt any emotional pain or fear as a result of an interaction with Randy, she would automatically turn her pain into anger and want to strike out at him. She had always been able to acknowledge her anger—but she had never looked beyond it to the next step: the destructiveness with which it expressed itself. Now Randy was also able to understand that it was Jackie's denial and especially her verbal abuse that had made him so angry and resentful of her so much of the time.

They could laugh together at last in discussing the wrangling over the car keys, a pattern they had played out many times before, but which had baffled them until now. When Jackie would start to feel frustrated, guilty, and fearful of losing Randy, she would unconsciously seek his reassurance in the only way she knew how: by threatening to leave, hoping that he would ask her to stay. He contributed to the maintenance of her dysfunctional behavior by unconsciously playing this game. Now that these actions and reactions were out in the open, it became clear that much of the destructive pattern of their conflict was rooted in Jackie's wounded early childhood and the frozen feelings that were triggered when she was at odds with the person she cared most about. Individual psychotherapy became the priority; couples counseling would have a much greater likelihood of succeeding after she had worked through some of the pain from past wounds.

WHEN TO WORK AT IT

In situations like Randy and Jackie's, once the partners realize that the relationship triggers early childhood traumas they must decide what their own limits are, how important the relationship is to them, and how much they are willing to invest in time and energy in working through such deep-seated issues. They need to have a plan, to decide at what point the negative outweighs the positive. If the relationship is of short duration and is not engaging, some people may well decide that it would be easier to find other partners who won't trigger the same kinds of echoes from the past; not all relationships raise the same amount of early childhood material. On the other hand, if other aspects of the relationship are fundamentally sound, if the partners are compatible and care deeply for one another, they may decide the relationship is worth saving and improving.

The range of personal discomfort people are willing to accept is also tied to their underlying beliefs about relationship. Some may believe the ultimate reason for being in relationship is companionship; others may believe it is security, romance, or a stimulus to personal growth. Any individual perspective is acceptable, as long as it is based on a healthy sense of self and an idea of what a healthy relationship is; some relationship addicts rationalize staying in destructive situations by using personal growth as an excuse. Adult children of dysfunction may have an underlying belief that you need to "work" on a relationship; what is actually called for is a *tending* of a relationship—as one would tend an orchard.

One form of reframing that often works for chronically conflictual situations is distinguishing between problems and difficulties.[5] Once you define something as a problem, you seem to go to the next step, which is that problems are there to be solved. Some difficulties defy immediate solution—though you might rather believe the myth that there is a solution for everything, if only you can find it. This myth appeals particularly to family heroes, the fixers who grew up with grandiose ideas about being in charge. But what kind of solution can there be, for example, when job changes beyond your control precipitate serious differences in personal, professional, or financial status between partners? What kind of solution can there be when an accident causes significant differences in level of health and freedom of action or movement? If both partners can look at the difficulty openly and share their vulnerability, they can join forces to make life more bearable for themselves and each other during the crisis, strengthening rather than undermining the relationship. When such difficulties become chronic, they may also force one or both partners to consciously acknowledge and grieve the death of utopian dreams.

LONNIE AND RON

Lonnie, a bright and successful real estate agent, gradually came to realize that her fiancé, Ron, would never set the world on fire. His job security was always tenuous, and he seemed to be in constant financial trouble. But she thought she could help fix the situation once they were married, so she went ahead with their plans. However, Ron's financial instability continued to create ongoing friction in the relationship. For a while Lonnie invested a lot of energy in trying to help him start a new business, setting up his books, telling him how to market his services, and so on. She saw the situation as a problem to which she had the answer, rather than as a chronic difficulty that defied her action-oriented solutions. Eventually she realized that this approach was gaining her nothing but anger and frustration, as well as a lot of resentment and resistance from Ron. She abruptly stopped trying to fix things for him. In therapy she came to recognize that underneath her obsession with helping Ron was a dream she had always had of being taken care of by a strong, capable man. She could give up Ron and keep chasing the dream. Or she could let go and accept this man, whom she loved very much and who in many ways was a very good partner and companion for her, surrendering and grieving the loss of her childhood's fairy tale dream. In doing so she would also need to accept the adult reality that ultimately, no matter whom she was in relationship with, she would have to be the one to take care of herself. Finally she would have to start exploring her own pattern of caretaking behavior and the motivation behind it.

In contrast to difficulties, problems are situations to which solutions *can* be found. But many problems can also be reframed. In that case, instead of a *solution* to the problem, there is a *resolution* of it. Nothing in the external situation has changed, yet a change in perspective (or a reframing) has dissolved the previous discomfort.

MO

Mo, a nursing student in her late twenties, developed a serious weight problem in the past several years. She had tried all sorts of diets, nutritional supplements, and exercise programs, but the problem persisted; nothing seemed to work. She knew her obesity had addictive qualities, and finally started attending Overeaters Anonymous meetings. It was the reframing of her problem from "I need to control my weight and I can do it" to the surrender of "I am powerless over food, and my life has become unmanageable" that made the difference. The paradox that you must surrender before being able to recover from your addiction is central to all Twelve-Step programs and carries in its wake the paradox that self-empowerment follows surrender. It is an effective form of reframing; *surrender implies that you accepted the way things really are*. Living in denial precludes the possibility of real change. Paradoxically, you find your own personal power when you give up control over people, places, and things.

LOVE, HONOR, AND NEGOTIATE

In some contemporary homes the familiar and quaint cross-stitched sampler is taking on a new twist. It says, "Love, honor, and negotiate." Negotiation is at the heart of conflict resolution through problem solving. The modern win–win concept of negotiation, in which there are no losers, has turned on its head the notion of winning as competition, which assumes that whenever someone wins, someone else has to lose. Whenever you speak of a win–win situation, you make a strong statement. You're saying no one wins unless everyone wins. This is as true of peacemaking efforts for the planet as it is for negotiation between partners.

RITA AND DAN

Rita and Dan have been married for twenty-two years. Despite periodic hardships and the common trials and tribulations of long-term relationships, they continue to enjoy each other and share a satisfying, mutually supportive and active life together in the small town where they live. Since their younger son left for college, they've spent more time together, enjoying their shared passion for boating and the sea.

Rita is a bright, competent business manager in a large corporation; she loves her work and is a natural at it. Six years ago she was promoted to personnel director. But for the next few years she felt frustrated, because she had reached the top of her career options in her company and in her hometown. She found out through a friend in another city that a large multinational corporation there was searching for a vice president of human resource development. The friend persuaded her to apply for the position—"just for the fun of it." The game became serious business when the board of directors selected Rita for the position over two other finalists, making a very handsome offer. Rita was elated. The only trouble was that Dan, although pleased for her, balked at the idea of moving three hundred miles away. He also had been born and raised in the town where they lived, and loved their home, where his parents, and their parents before them, had lived all their lives. And his family name had helped Dan to establish a successful financial planning business in their community.

For Dan, moving was completely unacceptable. As he saw it, moving would jeopardize two fundamental areas of his life: his sense of personal history and his business success. He feared he would lose himself. For Rita, *not* moving was completely unacceptable. As she saw it, staying would jeopardize her chance to rise to a new challenge, to stretch personally and professionally, to test her limits. She feared that if they stayed she would stagnate.

They had reached a serious impasse, for this was a core issue for both of them. They argued a lot; their level of conflict and stress rose dramatically. Rita complained that Dan was being unfair. She had spent many years assisting his business efforts, raising a family, being the helpful wife. Whatever happened to the idea of quid pro quo—wasn't it time he allowed her to have her turn? She pleaded with him to support her in taking this once-in-a-lifetime opportunity.

Dan complained that Rita was breaking her vows. She knew when they married that he loved his hometown, that he was planning to set up his business and raise their children there. He had always been supportive of her professional involvements. Whatever happened to the idea of commitment—wasn't it time she remembered her responsibilities to the family and avoided breaching the trust they had built over the years?

He pleaded with her not to destroy everything they had built, forcing him to start all over again.

This mutual guilt making went on for some time—until both Rita and Dan realized they were getting nowhere. For the first time they became afraid for their marriage; it dawned on them that neither could back down without doing harm to his or her own sense of self. Yet if they continued to stay polarized, they might end up going their separate ways.

Dan and Rita consciously forced themselves to stop looking at their predicament in terms of either/or, all or nothing. They brainstormed together, at first jotting down any kind of option that came to mind, sensible or not, just to give momentum to their creative problem-solving ideas. Eventually they narrowed their list to three realistic choices: Rita could move to the city and take the train home on weekends. Or Rita could move to the city and Dan could drive there on weekends. They ended up choosing the third alternative—made possible, in part, by Rita's new higher income: Dan would cut down his work to half time. Although they would still have to make do with a more modest way of life, Dan's reduced workload would allow them to spend four days together at their primary residence in the city, and Dan could still maintain his personal and professional relationships in his hometown. Keeping both households meant that Dan and Rita could also spend some of their weekends together in his family home, keeping old friendships and community ties.

When people's "bottom lines" are at stake, the primitive reactions aroused in defending the fundamental sense of self may seriously threaten an otherwise solid relationship. High emotions may also obscure available options and solutions. In Rita and Dan's case, both valued their own work as a central part of their lives; neither was willing to compromise her or his own essence and growth—even for the sake of a beloved partner. If Dan and Rita had not broken through their initial black-and-white thinking, they would probably have separated.

FIRM BOUNDARIES

People have intellectual, physical, and emotional boundaries that can be breached in different ways. Chapter 2 described firm personal boundaries, and respect for them, as a key quality of healthy families. Chapter 3 discussed the importance of boundaries that are firm without being rigid. As was pointed out, overly permeable personal boundaries are characteristic of relationship addicts and of children who were emotionally, physically, or sexually violated.

In order to create a strong love relationship, it is important for each person not only to know when and how to set clear limits but also to accept and honor the boundaries and limits set by the partner. As illustrated by Rita and Dan's story, these bottom lines are really expressions

The Zipper Metaphor

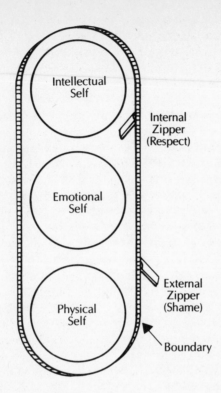

Figure 8
Source: Merle A. Fossum and Marilyn J. Mason, *Facing Shame: Families in Recovery* (New York: W. W. Norton, 1986), p. 71.

of self-knowledge, and can become the steppingstones to a sense of trust, safety, and acceptance.

Ideally, personal boundaries are best based on your own internal stimuli, not on a reaction to external cues. As expressed by one model, it depends where the boundary "zipper" is: on the outside, where it can be moved at will by others, or on the inside, where it is controlled by the boundary's owner.[6] (See figure 8.)

There is something empowering about setting and regulating the permeability of one's own boundaries. Realistically, this is not always easy to do, for situations can rush in that require us to take an immediate stance. When we are caught unprepared, we may go to extremes, putting up no resistance to someone's boundary intrusion, or shutting down emotionally, reacting rather than consciously choosing from the range of response options available.

Overly permeable boundaries pose a real threat to recovery for relationship addicts. Isolated slips in addictive behavior, which sometimes escalate into full-blown relapses, are more likely to happen when someone's sense of self (or personal boundary) is vulnerable. (Slip and relapse prevention are addressed more fully in Exercise III at the end of this chapter.)

In setting and maintaining firm boundaries, it is also your responsibility to communicate clearly what your limits are; it is only fair that your friends and partner have the opportunity to decide whether such limits are acceptable to them.

For example, incest survivors victimized as children may have tormenting flashbacks even as adults. Such experiences may limit how a woman wounded in this way may be able to relate sexually—even though she is now with a partner who was in no way connected with the sexual abuse. Although her discomfort is in reaction to a current external stimulus, it is actually a holdover from her past. She must let her partner know clearly what her sexual boundaries are, so that her mate may in turn look inward to ask whether the situation is acceptable. Such dynamics also apply to victims of rape—but the emotional wounds of incest are harder to heal. Unfortunately, boundary issues of this kind are not as rare as we used to think. They can become serious challenges or obstacles, given the special place sex occupies in love relationships.

SEX IN RELATIONSHIPS

Healthy sexuality is a source of sensual and physical pleasure. It can be an expression of trust, of love, of tenderness, of fondness, of creativity, of playfulness. Sexuality is a powerful form of communication—in fact, the more connected the relationship, the more likely that the expression of sexuality will have all sorts of subtle, perhaps unstated and frequently unacknowledged nonverbal communication purposes beyond the immediately obvious ones. People use sex as a physical outlet for stress, fear, or anger, as a way to deal with insomnia, as a fantasy to replace a harsher reality, as a form of escape from loneliness or a sense of alienation, as a way to avoid talking about unpleasant or uncomfortable feelings, and even as an unconscious way to control, manipulate, or punish.

This society tends to be overly performance-oriented; we may attach too much meaning to our own, or our partner's, occasional disinterest or lack of arousal. There is a natural ebb and flow in people's sexual needs and energy, which includes variations in frequency, tempo, and intensity. During periods of extra stress at work or at home, or while under the influence of an addiction, it is not unusual for people to be less sexual. Partners of compulsive gamblers who place their bets at the track, for example, report that their mates' interest in sex is directly tied to the racing season calendar. Such variations are like the weather: essentially changeable. Just as one would not draw conclusions about the overall climate of a place from experiencing two weeks' torrential rain or torrid heat, so one can't use unpredictable sexual cycles to draw conclusions about a physical partnership. It is the *overall* quality of sex that is the "climate" and the overall barometer of one's physical relationship.

Even when a sexual dysfunction does develop, it is usually not nearly as serious as the people experiencing it may believe it to be. And, paradoxically, the more the partners worry about sexual performance, the more likely it is that the difficulty will get worse. Many sexual dysfunctions respond to treatment in short-term sex therapy. On the other hand, if the experience of the dysfunction occurs only with one particular partner, this may be a clue that something is wrong in the relationship.

In a sexual relationship it is important for partners to identify what they communicate or—more commonly—what they *don't* communicate to each other about sex. Are their messages generally positive or negative? Are the levels of their communication congruent—that is, is the message the same verbally as it is nonverbally, or is the message mixed? (If asked, most people in relationship would say that sex is one of their priorities. Yet the same people often relegate sex to late at night, when they are tired from a long day—when they wouldn't think of starting any kind of meaningful project!) What topics are avoided because of fear or embarrassment? Sometimes more light is shed on potentially troublesome areas by noting the things that are not discussed rather than those that are.

Children of distressed families often receive a distorted view of sex. Parents may have appeared totally distant and asexual, or sex may have been associated with conflict and violence, with drunken nudity, with so-called inadvertent touching. Such homes almost uniformly fail to provide openness, honesty, and education about sexuality.

People may respond to similar sexual experiences in different ways. With the passing of time, with gentleness and patience, and with a willingness to get to know the other person better, there is the potential for partners to become more sexually compatible, building a climate of intimacy in which they feel totally free to express their sexuality and sensuality with one other. Because trust invites surrender, which is so important in a sexual encounter, it is trust between people that is the aphrodisiac—not drugs, alcohol, or romance.

QUALITY TIME

The amount of time people devote to their primary relationship relative to the total time they have available is often seen as a reflection of their commitment and the kind of priority that relationship—or relationships in general—have in their lives. Yet the issue of time is not a simple formula. In our demanding world there is a vast difference in the available time of, say, a bank teller and a bank chief executive officer—or of a single nurse in an obstetrics ward and a married obstetrician with a husband and two young children. More and more, because of the pervasiveness of two-career couples, there are also vast differences between the time needs and time availability of two partners. The obstetrician's time will be very limited. And whether her available quality time will meet her husband's wants and needs may be partly dependent on his own availability and involvement. If he is a teacher who likes to be home with his family in the evenings, has every summer off, and has several school holidays during the year, he may be less happy with his wife's time commitments than if he is an obstetrician himself—or a teacher who is passionately involved in grass-roots politics in his community, sings in a choir, and coaches the track team.

Like sex, time in relationships is also a double-edged communication medium. It can be used as a tool for the expression of caring and nurturing—or as an instrument of power and a shield against intimacy. In addictive relationships time may become a bone of contention between distancer and pursuer. Whereas in symmetrical, or balanced, relationships time is frequently negotiated, in the interaction that takes place in addictive and other dysfunctional relationships the distancer controls the relationship by controlling the time. These dynamics are well described in Isaak Dinesen's recollections of her famed relationship with the explorer Denys Finch-Hatton, so poignantly retold in the film *Out of Africa*. After a few days' visit on her farm, Denys would routinely say he had to leave for some pressing engagement elsewhere. Neither Isaak's cajoling nor expressions of disappointment had any effect; at times his engagements were simply pretexts he used because he felt a need to be alone. For Denys, time was simply not negotiable. It masked his deep distrust of sustained routine and tradition, which he regarded as snares that jeopardized his fiercely guarded freedom. Isaak, on the other hand, saw the situation in terms of her own needs—as a rejection of herself and as a fear of intimacy and commitment on the part of her lover.

Today we hear a lot about the need for quality time in relationship, and it is said that the average middle-class married American couple spends only twenty minutes of quality time a week together. Quality time *is* important to the health of a relationship, for it is time spent discussing not the routines, or facts, of the day or week, but rather sharing thoughts, concerns, and feelings.

At its best, quality time is leisure time, open-ended, without built-in schedules or endings. It is time in which events, communication, activities are allowed to unfold at their own pace, without specific structure or agenda. It requires nothing except a couple's willingness to be with each other openly, accepting and allowing whatever comes. Even though open-ended time may be a rare commodity today, building occasional leisure time into an important relationship is essential for its well-being.

For a couple with children at home, it may mean going away somewhere for a weekend without the usual compulsive traveler's checklist of "must sees" and "must dos," without telephone or alarm clocks, without left-over office work, without a stack of Sunday newspapers or headsets to hide behind, without a host of mutual expectations except openness of communication and feeling. Granted, such a weekend has a built-in end-ing—but within it, time can flow at its own pace, without interference from any external constraints. For other couples, leisure time may work better at home—perhaps deciding to clear a Saturday night or the fol-lowing Sunday (or both) of things to do or schedules to keep, doing, saying, and being only what seems appropriate at the moment the activ-ity, thought, or feeling presents itself.

RACHEL AND JERRY

When they first started couples counseling, Rachel could not recall ever experiencing quality time—or leisure time—with Jerry during their eleven-year marriage. Rachel was a recovering cocaine addict and Jerry had been a workaholic during their entire marriage. They spent very little time together; only rarely did Jerry even come home in time for dinner, and he spent most of his weekends at the office. As a result they had a distant, intensely conflictual marriage that was all work and no play. Jerry and Rachel had never learned to communicate openly with one another, and their two children were beginning to show symptoms of their dysfunctional upbringing in acting–out behavior and poor grades. Rachel felt victimized, helpless, and powerless; her anger, turned inward, manifested itself as depression. Jerry was under constant self-imposed tension, which he transmitted nonverbally to the children when he was home. When he was around they fought with each other constantly. Jerry yelled at them for being disruptive and at Rachel for not making them behave, and then used the children's fighting as an excuse to pick up, slam the door, and retreat back to his office, where he needed to deal only with a responsive and predictable computer.

As one of their first assignments in couples counseling, Rachel and Jerry were asked to make a list, working separately, naming three activ-ities they liked to do together when they first knew each other, and a second list in which they named three activities they would like to do together now. Then they were asked to compare each other's lists. In this way patterns began to emerge of positives they used to share that had been nearly forgotten—focusing as they had for so long on the conflictual, negative aspects of their relationship. By reacquainting them with the positive sharing they had in the beginning, the exercise also became a starting place for reconnecting in the present.

Even though some common interests surfaced, Jerry and Rachel need-ed to get to know each other almost as if they had just met. Despite their eleven years together, there had been practically no intimacy between them—in part because Jerry shunned emotional closeness, in part because Rachel's feelings had shut down due to her drug involvement early in their marriage. Their therapist realized that they would have to learn to spend time together slowly, one small increment at a time.

Their first "practice" quality time together was to be limited to no longer than an hour and a half. The person in charge would plan an activity, and the spouse would agree to participate for the allocated time. They flipped a coin. The toss put Rachel in charge, and she decided it would be fun for them to go out to a fine Chinese restaurant that had recently opened in their neighborhood.

This first experiment was a near-disaster from the start. Jerry made the evening miserable in every way he could. He scowled and wouldn't speak at all on the way to the restaurant. He made a scene because the table they had reserved wasn't quite ready when they arrived. He complained that the prices were too high, the food was too spicy, and the service was too slow. Their spontaneous laughter over the inane messages in their fortune cookies finally broke through their isolation and discomfort. When they left, Jerry reached out and put his arm around Rachel's shoulders, and they quietly walked home.

The next week it was Jerry's turn to do the planning. This time the assignment again called for spending the evening together doing something fun. Again, the exercise started out as a near-disaster. Jerry, disregarding the time limit, secretly made arrangements for a weekend babysitter. Once he and Rachel had driven off some distance from home, he announced proudly that he had made plans for them to be away for the entire weekend. Rachel became very annoyed, because she had already made plans for Sunday. Her annoyance turned to rage when Jerry told her that "as long as they were going away," he thought it would be nice to visit his folks in the next town. He had called ahead, and his mother was looking forward to their coming for dinner and spending the night. Rachel felt discounted and discouraged that Jerry had turned what was supposed to be a special time for the two of them into a utilitarian trip to see his family. She also felt conflicted; she thought she should have been able to show some appreciation for Jerry's planning. Instead she felt guilty for being angry at him for his unilateral decision making which, once again, had aroused her feelings of helplessness and powerlessness. When she tried to speak to him about it, it was his turn to be surprised. "But that's how I run my business!" he exclaimed. Rachel realized for the first time that Jerry knew only one style of relating, the one he used in his electronic systems engineering work. All these years they had spoken two different "languages," neither understanding what the other was saying.

Eventually, for all these false starts, Rachel and Jerry's experiments with quality time are starting to be more satisfying for both of them.

They don't have a common language yet on which to build unstructured intimate time, but they're able to string together more than just a few minutes and hours at a time.

FRIENDSHIP

When Jerry and Rachel reach the intimacy of quality time together, then friendship may also blossom between them. Kahlil Gibran asks, "For what is your friend that you should seek him with hours to kill? Seek him always with hours to live. For it is his to fill your need, but not your emptiness."[7]

Friendship is the cornerstone of intimate relationships. In Chapter 6 we will look at the many guises friendship comes in—including lovers who become friends and friends who become lovers. Friendship certainly is not a precondition for starting an intimate love relationship. And yet it is hard to imagine that over time any such relationship could evolve into a healthy, successful, loving partnership unless along the way it had developed a strong element of friendship. For it is in friendship that we find the essence of the unselfish, noncontingent caring for another that nurtures the strength and growth of the friendship—and the friends.

EXERCISES: RELATIONSHIPS IN *YOUR* LIFE

In reading this chapter and the vignettes, you may have had occasional glimpses of unfinished business or uncharted territory in past and present relationships in your own life. In this section you have an opportunity to do some of your own exploring. Whenever we are able to retrace the steps that had led us to stray into the forest, we are able to find the way out more easily the next time.

EXERCISE I: LOVERS PAST AND PRESENT

Make a copy of the Relationship History Chart in Chapter 2. At the top of column 3 place the name of your current or most recent partner. At the top of column 4 place the name of an important intimate other in your past. In addition to the questions in the chart, ask yourself these questions (although they are written in the present tense, apply them to your past as well as your current relationship):

1.a. What qualities and traits do I value most in my partner?
   b. What qualities and traits do I believe my partner values most in me?
   c. What qualities and traits do I value most in myself?
   d. What qualities and traits do I believe my partner values most in himself or herself?
   e. Is there a discrepancy in my current relationship between what I value about the way we are with each other and what each of us values about himself or herself? If so, is the discrepancy due to the addictive quality of the relationship?
       If the answer is yes, what specific action(s) can I take to break the addiction? If the answer is no, what specific action(s) can I take to reduce this gap?
2.a. In what specific ways do I consciously nurture this relationship?
   b. In what specific ways does my partner consciously nurture this relationship?
   c. Are any changes necessary on my part? If so, what specific action(s) am I willing to take over the next month to improve the situation?
3.a. What are three actions or statements by which I have let my partner know with *congruent* messages that he or she is important to me (In the past month, for your current relationship)?
   b. What are three actions or statements by which my partner has let me know with *congruent* messages that I am important to him or her (in the past month, for your current relationship)?

EXERCISE II: THE CONTENT OF COMMUNICATION

Earlier we discussed communication primarily as process. We talked about verbal and nonverbal communication and about the need for congruent communication styles. The *content* of communication between two people can also reveal the degree of openness, or intimacy, between them. Which among the six communication content levels listed best describes your current relationship (the one you identified in exercise 1)? Note that this exercise can apply just as easily to friendship.

Cliché conversation

This type of talk is the lowest level of self-sharing. You talk about trivial matters, either restating things everyone already knows, or detailing at great length insignificant details of your external life that illuminate neither you nor your listener. "Yesterday I broke one of my false fingernails and you can't believe the trouble I had finding someone to fix it before last night, which was really important because. . . ." (off on tangent for five minutes about what was important about last night.) "First I called. . . ." (ramble on for ten more minutes about various manicurists' scheduling problems).

Ceremonial conversation

This is the typical, almost automatic exchange about the weather ("These storms are sure unusual for this time of year!"), nostalgia about the past ("I remember in 1963 you could buy a pound of hamburger for. . . ."), or perfunctory inquiry about people's health, "How are you?" "Fine, thank you. And you?" Although the content may seem as desultory as in cliché conversations, this type of interaction performs the socially valued function of making a connection, albeit fleeting, with strangers or near strangers, such as the mail carrier, the neighborhood shopkeeper, the acquaintance at the bus stop.

Reporting "the facts" about others

With this type of talk you give nothing of yourself and invite nothing from others in return. You report gossip items, conversation bits, and little stories about others: "Have you heard the latest about Sally and Rhonda?" "You'll never guess what happened to John yesterday!"

Your ideas and judgments

At this content level you start to share something about yourself. You take the risk of telling your listener some of your ideas and reveal some of your judgments and decisions. "I would like to share with you my opinion about this subject." "Well, I see it differently; let me explain." "If it weren't for Martin Luther King. . . ."

Your thoughts and gut level feelings

If you really want others to know who you are, you must tell them about the butterflies in your stomach, the pounding in your chest, the tightness in your throat—not just the thoughts in your mind. "I am going home today, and I am really scared." "When I am with you, I feel very comfortable." "I feel resentful when I sense you're not listening to me."

Peak-level communication

This type of communication is characterized by absolute openness and honesty; it is an element of what we referred to earlier as congruence between the verbal and the nonverbal. "When I first came here I felt uneasy, like a fish out of water." "That's exactly the way I felt! I had no idea anyone else felt that way too. I appreciate your sharing that with me."

The content level of communication can often be successfully deepened to a more intimate level when at least one of the partners is willing to take the risk of becoming open and more vulnerable. Are you?

EXERCISE III: SLIP AND RELAPSE PREVENTION

In recovery, relationship addicts experience a sense of personal effectiveness, a "can do" attitude, until a high-risk situation arises. For relationship addicts such situations include (1) coping with negative emotions; (2) social pressure; and (3) coping with interpersonal conflict. If the person in recovery has developed the skills to cope with the high-risk situation, her sense of self-effectiveness will increase her future resistance to slips. Therefore it is important for you to identify your individual areas of vulnerability in each of the following four areas:

Trigger people

What are the looks, personal traits, qualities and style of people who tend to trigger your addiction?

Environmental clues

What specific situations have you had difficulties dealing with emotionally just before, during, or after a situation that triggered your unhealthy dependence or loss of boundaries?

Minidecisions

For two weeks monitor in a journal the subtle ways in which you may sabotage your own recovery. For example, do you find yourself driving down his street, though it's off the beaten track? Do you find flimsy pretexts to call her, though you swore to yourself you wouldn't? How much energy do you use up in trying to hold back, or trying to decide whether or not it's OK to call?

Physical state changes

What feelings make you obsess about your addictive trigger? What makes you feel needy? At what times? Is it loneliness, insecurity, depression, worry, or . . . .? Is it a need to control? Impress? Manipulate?

Although identifying your individual situational risk patterns—what alcoholics call slippery places—can in itself greatly boost your sense of personal effectiveness, the process of psychological inoculation against slips is complete only when you apply a problem-solving approach to your insights: find alternative behaviors to those of the past; stop reacting, and instead take action only after making thoughtful decisions, slowly arrived at.[8]

EXERCISE IV: THE RELATIONSHIP PATH

The scale that follows lists the relationship steppingstones identified in this chapter. To what extent are they present in your current or most recent love relationship?

1. Circle the number on the scale that shows where you rate your relationship now; your rating should be based on *specific* behaviors or situations.
2. Mark with an arrow the place on the scale where you want your relationship to be. Mark with a second arrow the place on the scale where you can *realistically* expect this particular relationship to move.
3. Finally, choose one item from the list that for you is a top priority. Think about what you can do to integrate it into your relationship, and consider discussing your wish with your partner.

Least   Most

1. Similarities

| 1 | 2 | 3 | 4 | 5 | 6 | 7 | 8 | 9 | 10 |

2. Ability to Deal with Change

| 1 | 2 | 3 | 4 | 5 | 6 | 7 | 8 | 9 | 10 |

3. Compatible Values

| 1 | 2 | 3 | 4 | 5 | 6 | 7 | 8 | 9 | 10 |

4. Effective, Open Communication

| 1 | 2 | 3 | 4 | 5 | 6 | 7 | 8 | 9 | 10 |

5. Effective Conflict/Anger Resolution

| 1 | 2 | 3 | 4 | 5 | 6 | 7 | 8 | 9 | 10 |

Least   Most

6. Effective Negotiation

1	2	3	4	5	6	7	8	9	10

7. Firm Personal Boundaries

1	2	3	4	5	6	7	8	9	10

8. Healthy Sexual Expression

1	2	3	4	5	6	7	8	9	10

9. Shared Quality Time

1	2	3	4	5	6	7	8	9	10

10. Friendship

1	2	3	4	5	6	7	8	9	10

The steps to healthy relationships identified in this chapter are by no means limited to love partnerships. They are foundations for any relationship that holds the promise of openness and intimacy—including friendship, the topic of the next chapter.

CHAPTER 6

The First Milestone: Friendship

Of all human relationships, friendship may be the most enigmatic—and the conditions for its birth most elusive. Special friendships have a heroic quality. The grief of Achilles over the death of his friend Patroclus changed the course of the Trojan wars; the conversion from enmity to friendship in the encounter between the Mesopotamian ruler Gilgamesh and the wild hill man Enkidu became a cosmic event; the friendship of Eleanor Roosevelt and journalist Lorraine Hickock survived several decades, long periods and thousands of miles of separation, and the inequalities of class, status, and wealth. A poet once described friendship as

the comfort, the inexpressible comfort of feeling safe with a person,/having neither to weigh thoughts/nor measure words but pouring them all right out just as they are,/chaff and grain together,/certain that a faithful hand will/take and sift them,/keep what is worth keeping,/and with the breath of kindness/blow the rest away.[1]

Although friendships are among the most important relationships in our lives, they are often the most neglected. They are the least acknowledged, written about, and thought about. In these hectic times they are often the relationships we nurture least and take most for granted.

What makes friendship so special? Writing nearly twenty-five centuries ago, Aristotle distinguished three levels of friendship: friendship based on utility, friendship based on pleasure, and friendship based on goodness—the goodness of both friends. In this third and most special of friendships, each person "loves the other for what [he or she] is" and wishes for the friend all that is good—for its own sake and without ulterior motive or reward, a description that is echoed by the Christian concept of agape, or unconditional love. Aristotle believed that an unconditional friendship would also encompass the element of pleasure, "for all friendship has as its object something good or pleasant." He wrote,

That such friendships are rare is natural, because [people] of this kind are few. And in addition they need time and intimacy; for as the saying goes, you cannot get to know each other until you have eaten the proverbial quantity of salt together. Nor can one [person] accept another, or the two become friends, until each has proved to the other that [he or she] is worthy of love, and so won [his or her] trust. . . . The wish for friendship develops rapidly, but friendship does not.[2]

The qualities of a special, close friendship are as timeless as Aristotle's words. In these days of rapid change and existential uncertainty, there can hardly be a more rewarding experience than a cherished friendship with a long history—one that has survived the ups and downs of two friends' lives and loves, joys and sorrows, differences and vulnerabilities. Barbara Ehrenreich describes her friendship with her best friend, "Joan," in this way:

We have celebrated each other's triumphs together, nursed each other through savage breakups with the various men in our lives, discussed the Great Issues of Our Time, and cackled insanely over things that were, objectively speaking, not even funny. We have quarreled and made up; we've lived in the same house and we've lived thousands of miles apart. We've learned to say hard things, like "You really upset me when. . ." and even "I love you."[3]

Those who have the good fortune to share in this kind of friendship have experienced the power of giving and receiving unconditional acceptance. For at various times true friends provide a safe forum in which to express half-formed thoughts and tentatively perceived feelings, offer shelter from storms in other areas of our lives, salvage our abraded self-esteem, and salve our bruised spirits.

A MODEL FOR PRIMARY RELATIONSHIPS

Close friendships are also good models for primary relationships—those special sexual relationships to which we attach our hopes for long-term, committed love partnerships. It is so easy for us to allow, and even encourage, our close friends to be true to themselves, to grow, to pursue their personal quests—so easy to believe in them and in the truth of what they tell us, so easy to affectionately tolerate their foibles. If only we were equally capable of overcoming our own threatened needs so that we might extend more of this kind of support and trust to our partners! In addition to a track record through hard times and good times to rival many a love partnership, special friendships like that of Barbara Ehrenreich and "Joan's" manage to nurture many of the qualities most precious in life, such as shared play and laughter, which so often dry up when we try to work too hard on serious relationships. At times we take those words *work* and *serious* too literally, substituting a certain humorless grimness for the healthy ability to laugh at ourselves and the vagaries of life and relationships. That grimness, that need to "make it right" at all costs is, after all, not too surprising among those who grew up in dysfunctional homes. As children they may have known no other way to survive a stressful family environment but through sheer determination and by damming up their emotions. This is what makes play, laughter, and tears such important elements in the reparenting process of the inner child.

Friendship has its own intrinsic reward; for Aristotle, close friendship is inseparable from intimacy—and certainly from the commitment of time, honesty, loyalty, and tolerance. In addition, because trust is the foundation that builds intimacy and commitment, one of the rewards of being a good friend is that the experience is likely to also make us more sensitive and caring love partners and life companions.

Still, despite the similarity in the qualities that make for both an inspired friendship and a successful primary relationship, sometimes we enter into sexual relationships with people whom we would not consider worthy of the investment of time and effort necessary for us to be friends—either before or after our involvement! It is equally true that we are usually not sexually interested in our close friends.

Paradoxically, however, just as trust, intimacy, and commitment are key factors in close friendships as well as primary relationships, so friendship is a key factor in all healthy, fulfilling love partnerships.

FRIENDS AND LOVERS

Friendship can be a way for us to heal some of our relationship issues without becoming sidetracked by the typical overlay of social preconceptions and emotional overload that can get in the way in love relationships. Whenever sex is involved, unconscious defenses, such as projection or projective identification, are often triggered—as in Paula's case (Chapter 3). By removing the excitement of the chase and pressure for sexual performance, the sexual neutrality of friendship avoids confounding and complicating the basic interaction between two individuals.

Adding sex to friendship—to any relationship, for that matter—inevitably changes the character of that relationship, which is another of those great unanswered relationship puzzles. The shift that occurs is more than merely a cultural bias; it seems to trigger a deep, archetypal human response. Suddenly expectations may change, demands escalate, and a new possessiveness and sense of ownership creep in. We are no longer seeking just the support and closeness of friendship, we experience that mysterious impulse to fuse and merge with the other that comes with being in love. Perhaps sexual encounters trigger a response similar to the undifferentiated infant's ecstatic union with its mother— a state we may unconsciously attempt to replicate all our lives.

This is not to say, however, that friends cannot become lovers. On the contrary, lovers who place liking before lust have a better chance to move from being in love to genuine love and intimacy than people whose encounters are based only on "chemistry." When a lover is someone we truly like and respect, it is also worth the effort to try saving the friendship once it becomes clear that a marriage or other primary relationship is over. No matter what the outcome, there is great value in the process of sorting through the relationship. Willingness to attempt this kind of transformation forces us to move from the corrosive effects of blame and recrimination into forgiveness, tolerance, and the acknowledgment that relationship dynamics by definition are the result of *both* partners' contributions.

What's more, in communicating with former lovers as trusting and trustworthy friends, there is much for us to learn about our own behavior in primary relationships. Once we step outside a love relationship—unconscious motivations no longer clouding reality—we may see clear patterns in behavior that had seemed to defy explanation or reason. Pam, a therapy client who had grown up in a distressed home where it was virtually impossible to trust, recently ended a painful addictive relationship with a partner toward whom at times she had felt quite ambivalent and whose love she had never allowed herself to fully trust. After some time apart she and Brian, her former partner, made a commitment to separate their friendship from the failed love relationship. In the process Pam was finally able to experience for the first time the truth that had eluded her earlier. On the day she and Brian ended therapy, she turned to him and whispered, "You know, suddenly I have never been so certain of how deeply both of us care for each other." Their laughter and tears mingled as they held each other—a welcome release that sealed the past and marked a new beginning.

KATE

Kate, a successful and assertive businesswoman in her early thirties, has been facing very different friendship issues this year. Since her teens Kate has had relationships with both men and women. Even though she excelled academically and as a student leader in both high school and college, it has always been difficult for her to be in touch with her feelings. Sharing her feelings with others has been even more difficult. Yet because she is determined to build a life with someone special, she is keenly aware of the importance of this level of sharing in relationship and has worked hard to become more attuned to herself and to express her inner experience in words.

While in her twenties Kate had several short-term relationships with men. Then, two years ago, she became involved in an on-again, off-again addictive relationship with a woman. Shortly after they started living together, an old flame reappeared in the life of her lover, Catherine, who felt torn between her two lovers and could not make up her mind. After a year of stressful ambiguity, Kate moved out and began setting some limits. Each time, Catherine would make new promises. But time after time the agreed-on deadlines would pass, and then would be extended, without anything ever being resolved.

Eventually, once she faced the fact that nothing was changing, Kate finally began to back off. In the past few months she has had only occasional contact with Catherine. She has managed to detach from the situation by disengaging emotionally. She has learned not to react to her former lover's ambivalent messages aimed at reengaging her in the old game. She has developed the strength not to initiate any contact, and responds to Catherine's phone calls only when it feels appropriate and emotionally safe.

Her withdrawal from a relationship to which she devoted practically all her time and energy for two years has forced Kate to face the void in her life. At a time when, more than ever, she needs support, caring, and a sense of community, Kate has no safety net of friends. Rather than building an open system of friendships, in the two years they were together, she and Catherine developed a primary relationship that, because of its narrow and exclusive focus, virtually isolated them from meaningful contact with others.

Fortunately Kate is close to both her parents. When she was a freshman in college, she chose to tell them and her two sisters of her attraction to both men and women. She cared for her family, and didn't want to keep an important side of her selfhood hidden from them. The family struggled with the new information for several months. Ultimately they reaffirmed their love for Kate by accepting her as she was and by respecting her own struggle to be true to herself. Despite their support, during her college years (and for a number of years prior to that) Kate's self-esteem suffered greatly. Sexuality is an important aspect of our identity as human beings. Yet many people who are either gay, lesbian, or bisexual grow up with a low sense of self-worth and shame, sensing that if they risk being open and give free expression to this aspect of themselves, they will be punished and rejected by everyone they care about.

In Kate's case, low self-esteem and her lifelong struggle to identify her feelings have been more in response to the oppressiveness of the environment than of her family. Our society still regards as suspect and unacceptable the emerging identity of someone who differs from the majority in any significant way—especially if that difference is related to sexual orientation. Such disconfirmation is all the more damaging to a woman's sense of self, which develops as a result of "self-in-relationship."

Kate's high school friends were attracted only to boys and were very vocal about their infatuations, but she was faced with the uncomfortable reality that from time to time she would also be attracted to someone of her own sex. Having to face this truth was both frightening and confusing for Kate, and she felt alone—as if she were the one person who was out of step with the universe. With no one with whom to share her feelings, she buried them and never learned to express them in words. Because it felt so threatening to reveal this side of herself, it was also difficult for Kate to form the same kinds of peer relationships as her schoolmates. She very much wanted to be accepted. She dated boys and, just like everyone else, necked in secluded lovers lanes. But this approach allowed her to express only one part of herself. She started feeling dishonest with both her friends and herself. She had to bear her pain and confusion in isolation and secrecy, because she felt there was no one she could confide in about her relationships with other young women.

Kate's adult relationship difficulties are a direct product of this backdrop. To survive, she learned to tune out and numb her feelings. As a result she also has trouble expressing them. Not surprisingly, Kate finds it difficult to know and express her needs and wants in relationship.

Every one of Kate's relationships has been marred by her need for self-protection. A part of herself is shut down, unable to find expression openly and spontaneously. With heterosexual friends and lovers, she has been reticent, reluctant to take the risk of sharing her sexual orientation with them. Her two sexual encounters with women in college were secretive and followed by a guilt-ridden flurry of male partners. Neither she nor the young women she was involved with ever discussed the implications of what had happened between them. Even her generally supportive family had made it known in indirect ways that they were uncomfortable with the details of this side of her identity. Although Kate has since learned to be more comfortable with her sexual identity, in her childhood and teens she missed both the validation of who she was as well as much of the intimacy of sharing secrets with friends that is part of the normal developmental process. To this day, these deep scars negatively affect her self-esteem.

When she began to think about friendship after the breakup of her relationship with Catherine, Kate came to realize that the way she knew to build close friendships was through her sexual connections: in the past all her meaningful friendships had been with former lovers. As is true for many people, sex for Kate seemed the easiest, most familiar way she knew to build any kind of close connection. For her there was an additional strong incentive for turning the women she had been involved with into friends—they were safe. With them she didn't have to lie, or struggle with the calculated risk of self-disclosure. Since making these discoveries Kate has been careful not to jump into a new sexual relationship just to fill the void left by the last one, aware of how vulnerable her occasional loneliness makes her. She has decided to trust in her ability to develop relationships with a potential for close friendship.

In reviewing her current social life, Kate also realizes how easily she had been willing to call people friends in the past. In one of her journal entries she asks, "Was I so eager for validation, for the warmth of human contact that in one single, giant semantic leap I would try to instantly bridge the gap between mere acquaintance and friend? Was this another variation of the 'all-or-nothing thinking' I've done in the past? Sex partner, lover, neighbor, well-wisher, alter ego, companion, playmate, confidante, ally, mentor, officemate, partner, comrade, pal, sister—Roget's Thesaurus, where were you when I needed you?! 'Friend' is special, a term for me to reserve for the handful of very special people whose presence in my life I can celebrate and nurture in a very special way by being a true friend myself. Now I finally understand the hyphen that author Mary Daly places in 'be-friending': it's the paradox of friendship—something dependably solid, yet constantly changing, becoming, transforming itself and the friends."

It has always been clear to Kate that friends have affected her life in important ways. She also knows she wants to choose her friends differently now. Having been addicted in several of her past relationships, she was very dependent and compliant, trying to change herself into whatever she thought her lovers wanted her to be. When, for a time, former lovers would become "friends," Kate would realize for the first time that the two of them had very little to talk about once they had finished their idle chatter about the movie or the dinner plans. Sometimes their values—the principles that guide, unify, and assign priority to life's choices, decisions, actions, and relationships—turned out to be diametrically different. Neither could understand the other's goals and dreams, nor accept and support each other's way of reaching them. More often, Kate was merely aware of what she could *not* support about her ex-lovers' ways of life or values, yet was unable to say what she could agree with, subscribe to, or enthusiastically support, because she had neither sorted through nor spelled out for herself where she stood on important issues. Having neglected to define her own values in life, she was incapable of defining them and herself in relationship. Only in the slow and painful separation from Catherine and the subsequent recovery process from her addictive behavior is Kate getting to know herself well enough to put her values—her bottom lines—into words. In turn, her values are guiding her in identifying her needs and wants. Kate defines her *needs* as those qualities and values so essential to her that she would not enter into another relationship without them. She considers her *wants* to be strong preferences that under special circumstances might be negotiable.

Looking back over the years, Kate thinks fondly of one particular friendship that she values above all others—and which has remained intact despite the two thousand miles, a husband, three children, and the suburban family life that separate her from her friend Marsha. Since their days in college, Marsha has always seemed to bring out the best in Kate, who finds herself empowered to respond in kind. Beyond the immediate pleasure of her company, Kate appreciates Marsha's complete acceptance of her lifestyle, her support of her career choices, her nurturing affection, and the intimacy they have developed over the years. At times they have dared to disagree on important points, because honesty has always mattered more to them than uncritical support. Recalling Marsha's occasional well-placed but gentle criticism, Kate sighs good-naturedly, "She doesn't always give me what I think I want, but she certainly always gives me what I need!"

Kate and Marsha share most values. And despite the gulf that separates their lifestyles, they have felt comfortable sharing their most closely guarded secrets and struggles, building a sanctuary of trust with one another over the years.

Kate has asked herself what, in addition to shared values, makes her friendship with Marsha so special, so different from all the others. Besides being a close female friendship that never included a sexual element, she recognizes that, perhaps because of the geographical distance and their different lives, she has never burdened this relationship with a lot of expectations. Yet, paradoxically, this friendship has met more of her emotional needs than any of the others. She has always felt totally accepted, and both Marsha and she have been emotionally available for one another in a pinch—spontaneously, by choice. "Perhaps acceptance, even more than shared values, is the true 'bottom line' of special friendships," she muses. "Now, once in a while I know the very first time I meet someone that I'd like them to be my friend—long before I know anything about their tastes or values. Maybe this happens when we read openness in their eyes, and an unspoken promise of acceptance for who we are."

MEETING YOUR OWN NEEDS AND WANTS

Like Kate, each of us at some point struggles to lead a more balanced life—a life that promotes our own growth and strengthens our personal relationships as well as our community ties. Often we look to our significant others to meet many of those needs. Each of us has some expectations of the special others in our lives. At the very least we expect to feel safe; each of us expects to be treated fairly, with respect, and with regard for our inner core. Usually we also expect to share the dreams and interests that make our lives worthwhile. At times, however, we also tend to go well beyond this point. For one thing, our childhood roles may get in our way. "Heroes" may want perfection in their relationships, and expect their partners to be perfect, never to snap, lose their tempers, or be in a bad mood. "Scapegoats" may try the patience of even the most tolerant of lovers with their acting out. "Lost children" may expect their lovers to read their minds. And "mascots" may expect their partners to make a joke of everything, as they do. Roles aside, there are many additional levels of expectation we have of our partners—unrealistic expectations that they will meet most or all of our emotional, social, intellectual, economic, sexual, and spiritual needs. When they don't we get hurt or angry, blaming them for our unhappiness. All along, our pain and anger act as red herrings that divert attention from the real sources of difficulties: ourselves. It is by focusing inward, rather than on others, that we find and transform the blocks to self-empowerment.

HOW TO MAP OUT YOUR OWN JOURNEY

When it comes to needs and wants, we are responsible for three things: first, we need to find out what both our needs and wants are, and how to distinguish between them. Next, we can begin to find out in what ways we are meeting, and can meet, many of these needs and wants ourselves—irrespective of what our partners choose to do. Finally, we also need to sort out legitimate, current needs from those blind, frozen needs that still haunt us from our early childhoods.

In one of her workshops, cathartic therapist Annette Goodheart invited a volunteer from the audience to talk about her frozen need for attention. With great finality Dr. Goodheart told the woman that she needed to give up any hope that it would ever be met. She went on to ask, "Now, if I were to guarantee that you'll *never* get all the attention you need, how would your life be different?" After a long pause, the woman answered softly, "I guess I'd have to decide to change it myself. I'd decide to be happy instead of sad."[4] She realized she had choices, that she alone held the power to change how she felt. We may be powerless to change the *circumstances* of our lives, but the *quality* of our passage is always up to us.

BALANCING YOUR LIFE

Leading a balanced life is the aim of most people on a journey to self-awareness and change. For a person who grew up in a dysfunctional home, and especially for a relationship addict, it means consciously starting to build a life that is rich in its many-faceted aspects, while removing yourself from situations and relationships that promote the roller coaster ride, the polarities, the highs and lows of emotional instability and excess. The world's great traditions have always advocated the balanced life. In the sacred Hindu epic *The Bhagavad Gita,* the charioteer/god Krishna counsels Arjuna, the spiritual warrior, to aim for *samaduhka-sukham,* the strength to have equanimity—that is, composure and evenness of temper—in both pleasure and pain. Likewise, the Roman poet Horace favored the life of the golden mean, the safe, prudent way between extremes. Excess was a central concern for the ancient Greeks; "Nothing to Excess" was the motto carved over the Delphic oracle's gateway. At the heart of Greek tragedy and blindly immoderate heroes such as King Oedipus lay hubris, arrogance toward the gods and the laws of nature that results from overweening pride and passion.

Leading a balanced life requires first and foremost identifying major areas in which you have needs, and then choosing means by which you can set out to meet them. To do this you must be able to name your needs and to distinguish them from your wants. It also requires that you know your inner core well enough to put your talents, skills, and predilections to work in ways that are likely to be fulfilling.

This sorting out may seem like a monumental and awesome task at first. Kate, for example, started out with only a faint idea of who she was, what things were *really* important to her, what she was good at, what she loved doing—let alone how to separate her needs from her wants. Slowly, through her work in therapy and her journal writing, by taking a "fourth step" inventory of her past relationships with her Al-Anon sponsor, by doing activities such as exercise III ("Your Inner Core") at the end of Chapter 3, and exercise III ("Thoughts and Feelings About Friendship") at the end of this chapter, and by tuning into her dreams and inner visions she began to get a clearer sense of self, of her interests and special skills, and of the things she valued most in life. Whenever she became discouraged she would remind herself of a quotation that had left a deep impression on her:

There are only two ways to approach life—as victim or as gallant fighter—and you must decide if you want to act or react, deal your cards or play with a stacked deck. And if you don't decide which way to play with life, it always plays with you.[5]

Kate came to understand that she had two different bottom lines—one that applied to her relationships and one that guided her life as a whole. Although acceptance was her single most fundamental need in relationship, her values were her overall bottom line. They were her life's priorities, the things she believed in so deeply that they became unifying principles that would guide her choices, her behavior, her decisions, and her interactions with others. For Kate these values included a commitment to her work, to integrity, to personal and spiritual growth, to service to the community, to family, friends, and other significant people in her life—and to balance.

IDENTIFYING NEEDS AND WANTS

Personal needs and wants fall into roughly six areas: economic, sensual/sexual, emotional, social, intellectual, and spiritual. Who meets those needs? How many are we meeting ourselves? How many are we expecting others to meet? What is reasonable? Taking a page from her business life, Kate decided to informally survey her current life's needs.

Economic needs

Kate included her basic physical survival needs in this category (food, shelter, clothing), as well as the financial resources she needed to meet her chosen way of life—housing, savings, entertainment, education, travel, contributions to projects close to her heart, and so on. She felt fortunate in this respect. Her needs and wants were well matched to her income and, unlike many other women, she had never felt she needed to stay in a relationship out of economic dependence. So in this area Kate was actually meeting 100 percent of her own needs. (See figure 9.)

Economic Needs

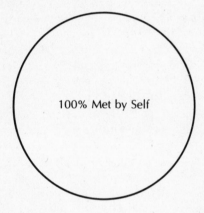

100% Met by Self

Figure 9

Sensual/sexual needs

Kate's recently ended relationship had met most of her sexual and sensual needs. Both being affectionate by nature, the two had been very free with physical touch and warm hugs. Now that the relationship was over, Kate missed the tenderness and sensual pleasure of physical touch as much as—and at times more than—sex. This was one area in which she felt very vulnerable. Even though she could choose to relieve some of her own sexual tension, to Kate, masturbation often seemed a poor substitute for the human connection of a meaningful shared sexual experience. Nor was her need for physical touch, for sensuality, being met—although twice-monthly massage and bodywork helped some. A little sadly, Kate acknowledged that in the sensual/sexual area, no amount of meeting her own needs could match the pleasure of sleeping cuddled against the warm, familiar body of a loved one. (See figure 10.)

Sensual/Sexual Needs

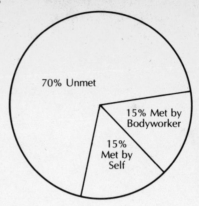

Figure 10

Emotional needs

Some of these needs were currently being met by professional associates and neighbors, by her family, and, Kate thought with a smile, even by her cat! The students in the business class she taught at a local adult education center were another source of emotional satisfaction, as were her therapist and her Al-Anon sponsor. But the lack of a love relationship and of close friends left a large gap in this area. Kate hoped that in time the people to whom she had started reaching out in friendship would enrich the emotional sphere of her life—regardless of what the future might hold in terms of a love partnership. (See figure 11.)

Emotional Needs

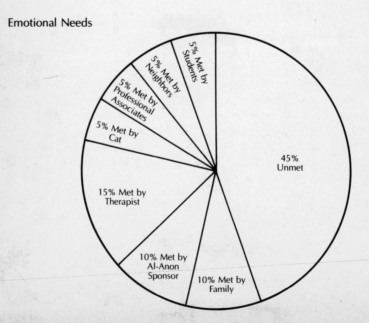

Figure 11

Social needs

This was one area in which Kate had no major difficulties meeting many of her own needs. She had plenty of acquaintances, colleagues, and pals with whom to socialize. She was also quite comfortable going to dinner, movies, and other public events alone. Granted that it was much more fun to do things with a special friend or lover, nevertheless, for the time being Kate was fairly satisfied with this area of her life. (See figure 12.)

Social Needs

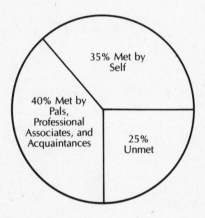

35% Met by Self

40% Met by Pals, Professional Associates, and Acquaintances

25% Unmet

Figure 12

Intellectual needs

Even though Kate could, and always had, met a large share of her own intellectual needs, she still missed the kind of in-depth conversations she knew were possible with a close friend such as Marsha or a partner like Catherine. Even though she attended workshops and lectures and was an avid reader, she realized that for her, stimulating and speculative dialogues were much more important. And for those to take place, she needed the opportunity, plenty of time, and an intellectual peer with whom she could safely let down her guard. For Kate, no such relationships were currently available, although some showed signs of moving in this direction. (See figure 13.)

Intellectual Needs

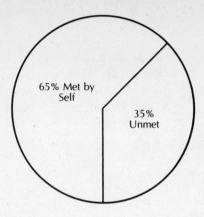

Figure 13

Spiritual needs

Recently Kate has met her spiritual needs primarily by regular partic-ipation in two Twelve-Step programs and by applying the Twelve-Step philosophy in her everyday life. (Kate defined *spiritual* as a sense of connection of her innermost self with others and the universe, a belief in something greater than herself—a greater whole.)

Both her work in therapy and the Twelve-Step programs also guided her to seek her spiritual center within herself through prayer and med-itation. Occasionally Kate still felt the gaping void inside. She knew that having close friends would help. At the same time she knew that no other human being—neither spiritual guide nor partner nor friend—could ever meet her spiritual needs. Others might support her journey and even point the way, as Kahlil Gibran suggested when he wrote, "Let there be no purpose in friendship save the deepening of the spirit." Ultimately, however, spirituality for Kate was an inner journey. (See figure 14.)

Spiritual Needs

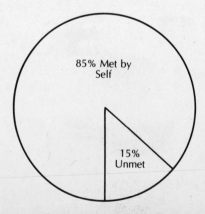

Figure 14

SEEDS OF FRIENDSHIP

Once she completed her informal survey, it became even clearer to Kate how much the addition of friends would enrich every aspect of her life. What's more, she realized that at that particular time the most powerful source of friends across all areas would be her Twelve-Step program groups, ACA and Al-Anon. What made these groups unique in terms of the potential for friendship were the members' shared values. These created a powerful unifying principle that cut across many other personal differences. And no matter how such friendships unfolded, there would be a foundation of shared spirituality.

Participation in Twelve-Step groups can be a powerful healing experience on several levels. Because it was impossible for people from dysfunctional homes to have their needs met in their families of origin, these programs' focus on taking better care of yourself and your own needs becomes a powerful reparenting tool. Some psychologists also believe that in order for people to overcome early developmental wounds, as adults they must find ways to experience and integrate three functions that many dysfunctional parents were unable to provide: the idealizing, mirroring, and twinship functions. Twelve-Step groups provide a powerful environment in which all three of these needs can be addressed.

The *idealizing function* is met early in life when a child can look up to a parent who, in the child's eyes, has some admirable qualities, who is able to soothe the child, and whose self-esteem is strong enough that he or she feels comfortable being idealized. Kate first started healing her idealizing function in therapy, where she could safely admire (and at times rage at) her therapist. When she began attending Al-Anon, she could also idealize the older, wiser members, who would share their experience, strength, and hope; they became models for her and a source of her own growing strength and hope.

The *mirroring function* is met in childhood when a parent mirrors the child's own feelings—whether it be the fear and pain suffered in a fall or the triumph of a gold star on a special school assignment. There is no more powerful mirroring for Twelve-Step group participants than looking up across the room, when they're sharing their experiences, to see a half-dozen nodding heads silently validating their own past pain or reinforcing their fresh insight. Describing one such ACA meeting, Kate recalled that she suddenly felt no longer alone, but understood and very connected—a vital element of the unit.

Twelve-Step groups are unique when it comes to helping people integrate their unmet *twinship* needs. The need for twinship—which occurs when the child proudly says, "I'm like you, Mom (or Dad)!"—is perhaps the most difficult need to meet in childhood if parents were emotionally unavailable or abusive.

Twelve-Step groups are safe forums in which to give play to twinship. Because they use a self-help format in which the facilitation of meetings is rotated among the participants, everyone is equal from the outset. A sense of twinship supports not only the growth and learning of newer members, but by saying, "We are alike," participants reduce their sense of isolation and strengthen their egos.

BUILDING FRIENDSHIPS

Suppose that, fresh from your beginners tennis lessons, you're the new kid at the local tennis club and are eager to improve your game. Your new court chums advise you to play "sideways" or "up," but *never* "down!" Their counsel makes you aware of an interesting dilemma: why would any player better than yourself want to play with *you?* So it's back to the backboards! Although it takes two to play, the quality of your tennis partners will depend on the quality of your own game.

And so it is with friendships. If someone were to ask you about the role of friendship in your life, chances are you would focus on the qualities of your friends—not on your own. Yet there is no type of relationship, not even a love relationship, in which like is attracted to like and mirrors back parts of the self the same way it happens in friendship. So whenever you are displeased with the lack of friends in your life or the quality of the friendships you do have, the searchlight needs to be turned on yourself—not on others. You might start by taking a look at your own commitment. All meaningful relationships, whether friendships or love partnerships, require a commitment of time, energy, and loyalty on both sides. One-sided friendships, in which one person gets most of the attention and support while giving little in return are common for adult children from dysfunctional homes. In their adult relationships—and friendship is no exception—they tend to recreate their family-of-origin model of the dysfunctional parent, who requires a lot of attention and energy on the part of the codependent enabler spouse. In Kate's case, being the relationship addict, she would usually pair up with lovers with whom she would feel she had to give much more than 50 percent. Even when ex-lovers became friends, she continued being the one who buffered their emotional pain, who was the loyal supporter of their views, and who was the good listener when they needed to discuss their problems. Yet these friends were seldom around when Kate needed support and caring herself. The commitment of time, energy, and loyalty was there, but it was one-sided. *The critical missing ingredient was the quid pro quo, or reciprocity, that is key to all healthy relationships of equality.*[6]

People sometimes find it difficult to commit time, energy, or loyalty to friendship. Yet for trust to develop, friends must be dependable both physically and emotionally. A promising acquaintanceship can grow into deep friendship only when both people care enough to make time to see each other, clear their emotional space to really listen to what the other is saying—in words and between the lines—and respond spontaneously and without calculation according to what is needed at any particular moment.

Recall Sarah, in Chapter 2. At one point she realized she had lost several friendships she really cared about because she had been so undependable and unavailable, canceling dates at the last minute time after time in favor of the man to whom she happened to be currently addicted. Sarah's renewed commitment to her friends became part of her recovery from relationship addiction.

THE VALUE OF FRIENDSHIP

Friendship is a gift that offers us the opportunity to experience intimacy and commitment in a safety net of mutual, unselfish caring. This can be of special value to people who grew up in distressed families, where friendships were discounted. In such homes friendships with "outsiders" were often discouraged, lest they discover the family secret. In addition, the family's denial and dysfunctional modeling of intimacy also made friendship, which requires openness, a virtual impossibility.

Unlike romantic love, many friendships last lifetimes. Perhaps because friends are so much more generous with each other's freedoms and so much more tolerant of each other's foibles than many lovers tend to be, friendships successfully weather life crises that would undo many love partnerships.

The sexual neutrality of friendship also allows people to fine-tune communication without the emotional overlay and overload that sometimes gets in the way in love relationships. There is no pressure for sexual performance, so it cannot confound the basic interactions between two individuals.

Above all, in friendship trust has a chance to unfold slowly; nurture, support, commitment are freely chosen, never becoming obligations. Friendship provides a setting in which people have a chance to observe the other person's real self and values in action rather than just in words. Friends can't "save" us, but they can certainly help us to save ourselves.

· EXERCISES: FRIENDSHIP IN YOUR LIFE

EXERCISE I. FRIENDS PAST AND PRESENT

Think of two very special friends. Place their names at the tops of columns 5 and 6 of the Relationship History Chart in Chapter 2, and fill in the blanks. In addition to the questions in the chart, ask yourself, regarding each friend:

1. What are the qualities and traits I value most in this friend?
2. In what *specific* ways do I consciously contribute to the friendship?
3. Can I name at least two actions or behaviors that demonstrate my commitment to the relationship?
4. Can I identify at least three actions or statements by which I let this friend know how important he or she is to me?

EXERCISE II. YOUR PERSONAL NEEDS AND WANTS

For each of the six areas of needs and wants described earlier, create your own pie chart in the style of Kate's. Regardless of whether you are currently in a primary relationship, identify areas where your needs are being met and not met. Sometimes this exercise yields surprising results: people find that more of their needs are being met than they had realized.

In areas where your needs are not being met, find constructive and creative ways in which you can meet more of them yourself. Review your pie charts: where and how does your friendship network support, enrich, and balance your own efforts?

EXERCISE III. THOUGHTS AND FEELINGS ABOUT FRIENDSHIP

Complete the following sentences that are applicable to you. Don't stop after just two or three answers—keep writing down the first thing that comes to mind until you've completed each appropriate sentence at least a dozen times.

1. My payoffs for having close friends are. . . .

2. My payoffs for having few or no close friends are. . . .

3. As a friend, the things I like best about myself are. . . .

4. As a friend, the things I like least about myself are. . . .

5. I prevent myself from making new friends by. . . .

6. I prevent myself from turning acquaintances into more intimate friends by. . . .

7. I reject offers of friendship or opportunities for new friendships by. . . .

8. In losing my friendship with (name someone who is no longer a close friend), I take responsibility for. . . .

When you have completed the sentences, review your writing carefully. What patterns does it reveal? What changes are you willing to make?

Although these three activities have focused on friendship, they can be used to explore loving partnerships as well, and are part of the path to love and intimacy—the subject of the next chapter.

CHAPTER 7

The Turn Away from Enchantment: Love and Intimacy

The tending of a love relationship requires a constant balancing act between our needs and those of our partner, our wish for togetherness and our wish for separation, our wish for belonging and our wish for independence. For that balancing act to be possible, we must know what we are feeling. More important, we must know the foundation, the source of those feelings: first we need to know who *we* are. To be intimate with someone else requires being intimate with oneself. Although we need to trust others, even more we need to trust ourselves—trust that we can be just fine, even if we are not in an intimate relationship, and trust that it's *in the loving*, not in the looking for love, that as a human being we are at our best.

SOME THOUGHTS ON LOVE

Over the centuries love has been sung, rhymed, idealized, eulogized, eroticized, operationalized, and romanticized, and yet love remains one of life's great mysteries. According to one view, love between relationship partners can be sorted into three basic varieties: instinctual, romantic, and conscious. From this perspective, *instinctual love* deals with the biological, physical expression of caring for another person; it deals with reproduction and sexuality. *Romantic love* is a fantasy of perfect, idealized love. *Conscious love,* is a commitment to a growth-enhancing relationship. Although all three types of love are necessary in the world, as we become more aware we move toward conscious love.[1]

Yet love partnerships at their best often encompass more than commitment, which is their rational, conscious component. They resonate to a spiritual quest in which, without being aware of it, we seek, as Robert Johnson has written, "to be possessed by our love, to soar to the heights, to find ultimate meaning and fulfillment in our beloved. We seek the feeling of wholeness . . . an experience of another world, an experience of soul and spirit."[2] This experience is not too unlike the experience of merger and boundary loss we seek when we are in love, or in an addictive relationship. It too requires a fine balancing act.

CONDITIONAL AND UNCONDITIONAL LOVE

It is only when love is neither romanticized nor addictive that it has a chance of balancing the inward journey of the soul and the outward connection of relationship. Then it has a chance of evolving into a conscious relationship in which both partners foster and nurture their own and their mate's growth.

Acceptance, not approval, is the foundation of real love. Yet on our path toward conscious relationships, most of us have repeated with our mates the patterns of conditional love we learned in our childhood and reinforced in our relationship addictions. What's more, we may not even be aware of the subtler conditions we attach to our love.

For example, what does the statement, "I'm proud of you" really mean? By itself, it is a support, a compliment, a positive reinforcement. But when it is the only or predominant way in which we compliment our mate (or our children, for that matter), it may betray—and communicate—a very conditional kind of love. The message may be, When you perform to my standards, I approve of you, I love you. Pride is a product of our ego and is usually associated with possessions—with ownership. Therefore, whenever we "feel proud" of another person, it is worth going inward to find out if we might have a sense of ownership about her or him, or if our boundaries are so blurred that we perceive that person as an extension of ourselves—an object to meet our needs for esteem, accomplishment, acceptance.

People also use conditional love as a prelude to, or justification for, control or aggression. Those three magical words, I love you, can become the formula under whose guise someone manipulates another into doing his or her bidding. The underlying message may be, Because I love you, I want you to change—or, Because I love you, I expect you to make things OK for me—or even, Because I love you, I know what's best for you. This is for your own good. That little word *this* covers the gamut of personal violations—from boundary intrusion to emotional, physical, or sexual assault. In each case the speaker is not really interested in meeting the other's needs—merely his or her own.[3]

The misuse of the word *love* to evoke feelings of duty, loyalty, or guilt frequently shows up in the bedroom. The more self-centered someone is, the more likely she or he is to whisper "love" to get a partner to give in and do something the partner otherwise might not. Likewise, the more dependent a person becomes, the more tempted that person may be at one time or another to say "I love you" to a sex partner just so she or he will say it back. Saying "I love you" or "I love him" can also become a rationalization, particularly for relationship addicts, to justify continuing to stay in unhealthy relationships. Women in relationships with addicts and batterers often repeat to puzzled friends and emergency room staff, "She's not like this when she's sober; besides, I love her," or "I know I should leave, but he's promised he will never hit me again; he says he loves me. He needs me."

They set aside the reality of their bruises, broken bones, and shattered spirits in pursuit of an ideal only dimly understood. They have not dared to ask themselves, What does love *look* like? How do I know when someone acts in a loving way? They have always been in such abusive environments that they know little about true caring. They poignantly hold onto a fairy tale world in which everything turns out well—despite warning signs and evidence to the contrary—ignoring reality's wry comment that sometimes things are indeed as bad as they seem.

The dishonesty that surrounds the word *love* is due not only to dysfunctional modeling and a wish to hold onto dreams. The erosion of the meaning of *love* is endemic to our entire culture, which supports and abets mixed messages. For some Native Americans, the words *I love you* mean "I will not harm you"—a very clear and caring message. Most of us, on the other hand, live in a culture and time in which love has been romanticized in order to sell products and institutions, and in order to maintain the status quo by the continued socialization of childlike, disempowered, dependent women. How much better it would be for us, both as individuals and as a community, if we were to adopt and extend the Native American understanding of love: "I will not harm you. As I share myself with you, so I will cherish, respect, and celebrate your separate, unique self."

THE LOVE TRIANGLE

According to one model, love can be represented by a triangle in which intimacy, passion, and commitment ideally make up one each of three equal sides. The more there is of each of these qualities of enduring love, the more love a relationship is likely to experience. In theory, the shape of a relationship triangle characterizes that relationship, highlighting areas of imbalance.[4]

For example, an unequal triangle in which commitment rules may betray a stale, tired, and perhaps rigid relationship, where little passion or intimacy is left and the partners stay only out of mutual dependence and insecurity. On the other hand, an unequal triangle in which the long side is ruled by passion may describe something more akin to an affair than a relationship. Given that it is short on intimacy and commitment, it is not likely to be growth-enhancing. (See figure 15.)

Sternberg's Love Triangles

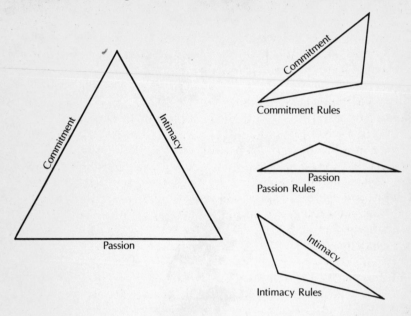

Figure 15
Source: Robert J. Trotter, "Three Faces of Love," *Psychology Today*, September 1986, pp. 46-47. *Reprinted from Psychology Today Magazine.* Copyright © 1986 American Psychological Association.

INTIMACY

Intimacy—the open sharing of feelings in an atmosphere of trust, acceptance, mutuality, and reciprocal empathy between equals—is surely the most tantalizing and challenging of these three qualities of love. Not only is much inner work and interpersonal practice required but, like a seedling in an arid environment, intimacy must grow and survive in a social setting that lacks and fails to support the qualities of intimacy. Our social lack of intimacy is rooted in our tacit tolerance of inequalities and the age-old climate of dominance–subordination between men and women, in how we value our relationships, and in our prejudices—that is, in our unwillingness and inability to create a safe climate in which differences are accepted and allowed. These attitudes often result in the oppression of those who are either perceived as subordinate in the power game, or as having cultural customs and lifestyles that differ from those of the dominant majority. And yet as one psychologist aptly put it, "Just because a plane falls out of formation doesn't necessarily mean the formation is moving in the right direction."

The AIDS crisis provides a useful insight into our society's current struggle with intimacy. In recent years a number of women who thought they were in committed monogamous heterosexual relationships found out that this was not so when their husbands or partners contracted either AIDS or ARC (an AIDS-related condition) through sexual activity or I.V. use. For one thing, such situations dispel the myth that being in a long-term heterosexual relationship makes you safe from AIDS. This myth is based on the mistaken notion that heterosexuality and homosexuality are two diametrically opposed polarities. In fact, sexual preference expresses itself as a continuum, as shown in the well-known scale developed by the Kinsey research team. (Appendix 11 is an adaptation of the scale.) Above all, the situation that is created by the sudden discovery that a heterosexual partner has AIDS is a reflection of a general lack of intimacy, a discomfort with being open in love partnerships, a fear of telling and hearing the truth in light of society's taboos, an inability to share feelings and live congruently—which means building trust by being honest, standing behind one's actions, and taking responsibility for personal choices.

JUDY AND MARK

Judy and Mark had been married for nearly fifteen years when Mark started getting chronic respiratory infections and debilitating bouts with influenza. The fact that he was a nurse and knew what he needed to do did not seem to help. After eight months of intermittent illness, Judy began to suspect that Mark might have AIDS. When she asked him, he flatly denied it, and became very angry at her for even considering the possibility. Months later, however, when he had become so ill that he had to be hospitalized, Mark finally acknowledged that over the years he had been involved in three same-sex affairs. Because of his "fear of hurting her," he had never told her—not while the affairs were happening, not when they were over, not when she asked. Mark had a strong personal denial system. He had grown up in a dysfunctional home, where denial was automatic—it was more comfortable, easier than the truth. Yet it was this denial that kept him from any deep intimacy in his life. Because he never understood who he was, he could never share with Judy his true self. He walked through life and his marriage playing a variety of roles, never able to assimilate meaning for himself from his life's experiences.

COMMITMENT

A commitment is a pledge, a promise that gives expression to your intent. In traditional marriage vows the words "till death do us part" are a commitment to stay together for life. In today's changing society, this ultimate relationship commitment no longer fits many people's reality. For one thing, the average lifespan is much longer than in the past. A commitment for life may mean living together forty years longer than

Maslow's Hierarchy of Needs

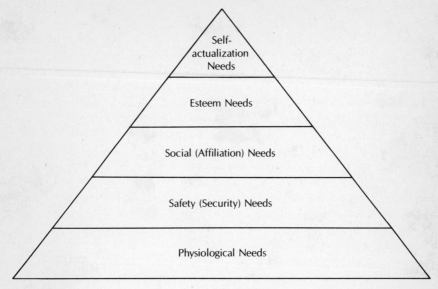

Figure 16

Source: Abraham Maslow, *Motivation and Personality* (New York: Harper & Row Publishers, 1954).

married couples did in medieval times, when such vows originated. Today both men and women have many more choices and opportunities to grow than they did even thirty years ago. Although this helps to make relationships potentially more interesting and varied, it also subjects them to additional stresses from periods of uneven growth between partners and from external challenges to unity of interests and purpose. Finally, the traditional "for-life" marriage commitment has less survival value in an urban, high-technology society in which our basic physical needs are met, in which brute strength no longer has major adaptive value, and in which a number of women are choosing to work and function autonomously and successfully apart from the nuclear family. It also follows that in this late twentieth-century environment, characterized by rapid changes, people's relationship needs are also different. If we look at a comparison of committed relationship needs in terms of Maslow's hierarchy of needs (see figure 16), it is easy to see that for most of history—and for most human beings—such relationships were essential for meeting basic survival needs (physical and safety/security needs), for the protection of the weak by the strong, and for the division of labor.

Although for most of the planet's populations these conditions still prevail, many First World people are now in a position to look beyond these first two levels of need. They seek to make commitments to satisfy needs at the higher end of the hierarchy—the social/affiliation, esteem, and self-actualization levels. They long to make commitments that underscore the special qualities of a relationship. Having watched many of their families' and friends' long-term, committed relationships and marriages break up despite traditional vows, a number of people are also starting to question the definition of relationship commitment and the assumptions and premises on which it is based. They are asking themselves the real meaning of commitment, trying to identify what it is that they can commit to wholeheartedly. This process requires going inward to ask what you can truly live by and carry through.

One difficulty comes from confusing intention and commitment. When you love someone and want to share your life with that person, you experience intention. At such moments you may well intend to live with the loved one for the rest of your life. But commitment is more than intent. It is a pledge to follow through to the best of your abilities, to honor the values that produce intimacy even during the most difficult of times. Therefore true commitment is not about "always" or "forever." Commitment is about staying power—about choosing to act responsibly in hard times as well as good times, in pleasure as well as in pain, and to honor mutual trust and loyalties at all times.

The commitment is to a process, a way of approaching intimate relationships. Any other kind of commitment betrays an unrealistic belief that you can predict your own and your partner's changes over time and how the interaction of such changes will affect your relationship, your needs, and his or her needs. When you commit to "forever," you echo the relationship addict's typical surrender of self to another. You place yourself in unpalatable Catch-22 situations: if in time the relationship no longer allows you room to grow, you must either break your promises or let your inner spark die.

CRAIG AND MARTY

Marty and her fiancé, Craig, each wrote a statement of commitment when they married, both for the second time. She wanted to be with Craig for the rest of her life, but she had learned some painful lessons from her divorce. She did not want to promise anything that someday she might not be prepared to adhere to. Instead she made a commitment that, even if she ever felt she could no longer preserve an intact sense of self within her marriage, she would not leave in the heat of anger, passion, or frustration. She pledged to stay for six months longer, no matter how difficult or painful a problem might arise. (Exceptions would be any situation that she might experience as abusive and/or unsafe.) During the six months she would try to the best and most sincere of her abilities to resolve with Craig the differences that seriously threat-

THE TURN AWAY FROM ENCHANTMENT / 143

ened their relationship. If they could not resolve these differences, Marty pledged to stay in open contact with Craig until they could make a gentle, caring ending with one another, avoiding blame, consciously acknowledging the good and valued aspects of their connection, and forgiving one another.

ANNA AND CRUZ

Another couple, Anna and Cruz, chose to express their mutual commitment in terms of process rather than time. Each pledged to make herself or himself readily available to the other, should they experience difficulties that jeopardized their live-in arrangement. They agreed to discuss their difficulties openly, carefully avoiding denial by staying open to the possibility that either one's interpretation of a situation might be a projection. They agreed to seek out the truthful opinions of trusted friends and a psychotherapist, and to give fair weight to factual evidence, not just to their emotions. Although the word *intimacy* may never come up in these situations, an honest and realistic commitment is built on trust, thereby fostering intimacy.

Monogamy

The monogamy/nonmonogamy issue can become a deadly tug-of-war in long-term relationships. It is an area of conflict that is often merely a symptom of much deeper-seated and often unconscious unresolved issues of intimacy, power, and control in and between partners. According to one study, for example, 72 percent of women who had extramarital affairs reported they did so because of emotional dissatisfaction with their husbands, and 39 percent said they felt naturally polygamous. A full 30 percent said they did not know why they had an affair![5] Besides reflecting issues of personal freedom, independence, or power, some people's reluctance to commit sexually may be a clue to a deeper discomfort with making any kind of commitment to another person. Because of the many psychological undertones of monogamy, there is a wide gap between people's actual behavior and the traditional biblical standard of sexual faithfulness which they pledge to uphold in their marriage vows.

According to recent surveys, for example, the percentage of married women who have extramarital sex ranges between 50 and 69 percent at the high end and 21 percent at the low end—depending on the study.[6] In any case, no matter which survey is quoted, the percentage of extramarital affairs for husbands is always higher than for wives. Given the high incidence of extramarital affairs, it is questionable if a pledge of absolute faithfulness is realistic for many—though their intent may be genuine. As is true for relationship commitment, the acceptable degree of sexual commitment may be worked out best by each couple individually to suit their common goals, their individual levels of self-esteem, and the meaning they attach to the expression of sexuality outside the relationship.

Monogamy is best viewed as a range, and the challenge is to find a partner who has views of monogamy similar to your own or whose differences can be tolerated because they do not threaten your sense of self.

JOSH AND LEAH

Leah, married for six years to Josh, is very aware that she would consider having an affair only as a form of retaliation if she were angry at Josh, or if she were truly unhappy in her marriage over a long period of time. If she were to break her commitment to monogamy, it would be an expression of her deepest feelings about her relationship. At the same time, she knows this is not so for Josh, who had a brief affair during one of his long business trips. Despite the momentary hurt she experienced when Josh told her, she understood that for him that sexual encounter was a temporary, if incomplete, substitute for the warmth and closeness they shared in their marriage. His slip from absolute monogamy did not threaten their relationship. Paradoxically, in fact, it strengthened their bond. Their ability to openly discuss this isolated incident reestablished and underscored their strong trust in the willingness of each to accept the other's vulnerabilities.

TANYA

On the other hand, Tanya, a homemaker in her late twenties, loved her husband and wanted children and a family. But three years after she was married, she ran into the man who had been her great love throughout her college years. She realized she loved both him and her husband, and she wanted to try to express her caring and attraction for both. Tanya was not interested in an affair with her former lover; she wanted an emotionally meaningful, satisfying relationship both within and outside her marriage, with the full knowledge of both the men in her life. Her husband was willing to try. Over time, it was Tanya who gave up this dream as unrealistic. Her experience taught her that the quality time she had available was too limited to experience and express the special qualities she had hoped for with both her husband and her lover. She reaffirmed her exclusive commitment to her marriage partner.

PASSION

In the triangle model of love, passion is defined as an emotion that "leads to physiological arousal and an intense desire to be united with the loved one."[7] Although we think of passion as an exciting, desirable, alluring part of love, ironically, its original meaning is to suffer, to endure—a feeling not too far removed from the condition of the romantic lover or the relationship addict. But when a healthy intimate relationship is also passionate, that is indeed a wonderfully enriching and pleasurable experience.

In long-term relationships passion and sexual energy have a natural ebb and flow. Although it has great regenerative capacity, at times passion may disappear, even in the best of relationships. At such times you need to have the ability and willingness to surrender to circumstances without trying to force your will on them. Believing that sexual passion can only be expressed through sexual intercourse is a very narrow view. Sexual passion is much greater than that. Intercourse is just one aspect of intimacy, and only one of the variety of ways in which partners give one another pleasure, and only one part of their overall physical relationship. And although it helps to accept that sex can change over time, it is still natural to expect sex and passion to be integral parts of a healthy love relationship.

RITA AND DAN

Rita and Dan, the couple introduced in chapter five, have had a passionate relationship over the years. Both knew from the night they met at a friend's home that their mutual attraction was worth exploring further. Over the following weeks they met several times for dinner, getting to know one another's interests and background, discovering their mutual love of the outdoors.

It was on their first outing into the wilderness that they began to open up emotionally to one another, and it was here that they first experienced the powerful sexual energy between them that was to be such a joyful aspect of their future relationship. Even though they laughingly acknowledged their mutual physical attraction, that day they did not act on it. Rita was accustomed to wait for the man to make the first move. Dan, despite his deep attraction to Rita, was reluctant to become sexually involved so quickly, having recently become aware of his destructive past history of sexual impetuousness that had led to a series of brief and emotionally unsatisfying affairs. When he met Rita he had been celibate for more than six months.

Eventually it was Rita who risked taking the initiative, one night several weeks later, when they were roasting chestnuts over an open fire. By then time had done its healing work for Dan. To her delight, she found Dan to be a sexually sensitive and responsive partner.

As they began their new relationship, Rita and Dan discovered a natural sexual compatibility. Both were free of sexual guilt, and their lack of interest in playing out socially "appropriate" sexual roles allowed a flowing, open expression of their sexuality according to the ebb and flow of each person's own inner range of masculine and feminine energies. Their willingness to experiment and eagerness to listen to each other's words and body language made them well attuned to one another's emotional states. These qualities made for a playful, joyful sexual relationship. In this setting Rita found it possible to explore her own sexuality even more freely, with fewer inhibitions, discovering in herself an inventiveness and receptivity that allowed her and Dan access to new, previously unsuspected sources of pleasure.

Because Dan and Rita were so aware of each other's emotional and physical states, neither felt a need to press for sex when one or the other's sexual energy was low or diverted by other priorities at work, at home, or in the community. They learned to be open about such situations—they refused to fake interest, and neither tried to hide their true feelings. These sexual cycles were not a threat to either of them; each knew that the deeply satisfying nature of their sexual relationship was qualitative—it had little to do with frequency.

During the many years of their marriage, Dan twice experienced erectile dysfunction. They barely took notice; Dan's self-concept as a man was not dependent on his physical virility. Together they had found so many satisfying outlets for their sexual and sensual playfulness that intercourse as such seemed almost incidental.

At times it was Rita who would go through stretches of disinterest in sex—usually because of stress at work. Although they had no sexual contact during such periods, they never stopped showing their affection for one another through other forms of physical contact. They kept cuddling, hugging, and holding one another. Occasionally conflict between the two of them would also interfere with their sex life. At such times they were able to allow each other the time and space needed to freely move closer again.

As their overall relationship deepened over the years, so did their sexual connection. From time to time a special moment of vulnerability or a flash of insight into a facet of the other's self would bring about a renewal in Dan and Rita's sexual relationship and in their love for one another. The openness and intimacy that unfolded at such moments went well beyond the sexual and filled them with a sense of awe. It was a communion of body/mind/spirit in which they felt united yet separate. Even after many years this special level of intimacy continued to permeate their overall physical and emotional relationship with a sense of wholeness, gentleness, and spiritual connectedness.

Shared Passions

When passion in a love relationship is spoken of, almost automatically most of us think of sex. But the word *passion* can also have different meanings. Other kinds of passion besides sexual passion are one of the common strands that run through successful relationships. Passion, in this sense, is the kind of common zest, enthusiasm, or fondness that two people in an intimate relationship feel for an absorbing project, hobby, or special interest they share. Amid the many social forces that tend to separate contemporary couples, a shared passion is a quality that often cements a relationship in positive, creative ways. Dan and Rita's shared passion has been their love of boating. Ethel and Frank share a passion for their grandchildren. They travel across the country several times a year to keep up with the uniqueness of their growing years. They lovingly tend their scrapbooks filled with finger paintings and photo albums overflowing with snapshots of birthday parties and other special occasions. For Nina and Louise, the shared passion is their common Twelve-Step tradition and the shared spiritual practices to which it has led them. In our society, which prizes the accumulation of tangibles, couples may also share a passion for collecting—be it Chinese snuffboxes, exotic recipes, crystals, or stocks and bonds. Again, it is not so much the content that matters, but the process—the function of the shared interest in providing a common bond, a source of mutual satisfaction and renewal.

TONY AND GABRIELLA

Tony and Gabriella's original passion came from sharing the rewards of raising Charlie, their only child, born six years after their marriage. By then they had nearly given up hope of becoming biological parents. This common bond kept them engaged for several years, but as Charlie grew older and more independent, Tony and Gabriella became increasingly aware of the void in their individual lives. For a while they each went their separate ways. After a few years, however, they ended up finding a spiritual tradition they could share. Since then their shared spiritual practices have become the foundation that sustains their caring relationship. The two of them come from very dissimilar backgrounds, with deep-rooted differences in attitudes, values, and expectations, and there is very little sexual energy between them. They freely acknowledge that without this shared passion their marriage would probably not have survived.

LOVE

What, then, is love between intimate partners? Is it something that can be fully defined in terms of a taxonomy of levels? Or of its identifiable component parts? No single definition would do justice to the term, because genuine love is something beyond what words can capture. Perhaps that is why the most engaging definitions have come from poets, whose every word—like Scripture—resonates with myriad allusions, connections, and levels of experiential understanding. A Chinese ideogram comes close to capturing this synergistic quality of love: "Love is the life force breathed into the heart/mind of harmonious human relationships."

And yet it is necessary for each of us to identify, each for ourselves what it means for us to love or to be loved, so that we can begin breaking the cycle of addictions, social myths, and empty and often manipulative uses of this most power-laden word in our language. Love is easily confused with other fleeting feelings, such as lust, infatuation, and even sentimentality—a few tears that are shed in the strong emotion of the moment, but that produce neither lasting insights nor lasting changes.

Real love is steady, consistent, enduring. Because of the romantic myths and exploitation that surround the word *love*, and the frequent lack of appropriate modeling, as adults we may have to learn all over again how to love. Fortunately we have the opportunity to do things differently. Real love is neither attachment nor a search for someone to love *us*, despite Tristan's "Oh, will I never find someone to heal my unhappiness!" As one keen observer has quipped, "Whenever someone tells me they can't live *without* a person, I know they can't live *with* them."

Love is something that can only be reflected back to us when we give it. Love loves through us, once we have found it within ourselves. "Your task is not to seek for love, but merely to seek and find all of the barriers within yourself that you have built against it."[8]

At its best, love between partners parallels the love between "good enough" parents and their children and the love found in the most inspired of friendships. It offers acceptance of and respect for the other's core, along with a desire and willingness to support and enhance his or her life without sacrificing our own core self. It pledges to encourage our intimate others to be all that they can be—even if that takes them far from us. In short, we commit ourselves to act only on our highest motives, no matter how much our own wants may protest. We act in a loving manner when the spiritual growth, satisfaction, and well-being of another become as significant as our own—and when, with our deeds as well as our words, we lend our support and encouragement to another even at the cost of our own comfort. Perhaps, paraphrasing and expanding the Chinese definition, we might say that love is the expression of an inner harmonious resonance so profound that we are able to transcend our own selfish motives to act in a truly loving manner toward others. This kind of love is the true point of healing contact between two human beings who come together in openness, hope, and goodwill.

EXERCISE: LOVE IN YOUR LIFE

EXERCISE I: YOUR LOVE TRIANGLE

Using Sternberg's model (see p. 139), draw a triangle whose sides reflect the character of your current or most recent love relationship. Describe in concrete, specific terms the steps that you and your partner might take (or might have taken) to make the triangle more balanced, in terms of commitment, intimacy, and passion.

CHAPTER 8

The Gift of the Path: Recovery

Leaving the enchanted forest of addictions is a milestone to be celebrated forever after—lest we forget. The ever-increasing distance and detachment we must place between ourselves and the addiction is built only in walking our new chosen path consistently, day after day, step by small step.

As with life itself, recovery is an ongoing, constantly unfolding, never-ending process toward wholeness and connection with self and others. In order to experience love and intimacy, first we need to put our addictions behind us and develop enough self-awareness to begin the discovery of who *we* are. Like divers in search of treasures buried on the ocean floor, we have to go deep to recover—that is, to reclaim—our true selves. Philosopher Sam Keen writes,

Yes, I would like a drink, but I want to remain clearheaded. Yes, I would like to go to bed with you, but I have promises to keep and miles to go before I sleep. The illusion of addiction depends upon keeping the multiplicity of our desires unconscious. When I invite all that I am into awareness I realize that no one substance, activity, or person has the capacity to satisfy me fully. I leave aside the security of the fix and begin the adventure of falling in love with the multiplicity of the self and the world.[1]

Relationship with self and others is at the core of the journey of recovery, for love relationships provide us with a learning lab filled with opportunities to practice life's lessons and experience personal expansion and growth. As we become more intimate with ourselves, our relationships with those we love improve. Conversely, the openness, empathy, and trust of a loving, intimate partnership invites self-inquiry. It can help us to practice what we have already learned, deepen our self-knowledge, and provide new lessons.

The process of recovery requires willingness. It requires the willingness to allow—that is, to let situations take their natural course without interfering, without trying to control, and without putting up walls of defense and denial. It requires the courage to witness what *is* rather than what we believe could be or should be.

Above all, recovery requires the willingness to accept temporary discomforts of change: the experience of chaos when old familiar patterns are swept away and new ones are not yet in place; the fear of being abandoned and rejected once we commit to being true to ourselves; the anxiety and panic that arise when we risk finding out what it's like to be really alone; and the new, fuller range of conflicting emotions we may allow ourselves to feel for the first time in our lives.

Finally, it requires the willingness to turn our eyes inward for answers to our difficulties, rather than outward to convenient scapegoats. Our willingness is incomplete until we can ask ourselves: "What is *my* role in this situation? How did *I* elicit that response? What could *I* have done differently? How do *I* keep myself stuck? What is *my* payoff in this? What traces do I see *in myself* of the traits and behaviors I claim to dislike so much in her or him? How could *I* have been more loving? How could *I* have made a difference?"

Technology has extended our outer limits. Electron microscopes have extended our eyesight to our physical inner space, sophisticated antennae have extended our hearing to the far reaches of our galaxy, computers have greatly increased the speed and power of our brains, complex robotics have helped us extend our limbs into ocean depths as well as sidereal space. *But we are just beginning to expand our inner limits, and that is the current challenge of the human spirit. It alone holds the promise that we may, at last, become cycle breakers, interrupting generations of family and social myths, dysfunctions, and conflict.* Then, each in our own small way, we will contribute to the numbers of people who choose to live in harmony. We cannot separate our private lives from the life of the community. It makes little sense to hope for peace on a planetary scale, unless we learn to live in peace in our relationships as individuals. The planet, after all, is not an abstraction, but a place made up of multitudes of individuals engaged in myriad interconnecting networks of personal communications, relationships, and systems.

THE EARLY STAGES OF RECOVERY

Turning our attention to ourselves and our focus inward is particularly important in early recovery, a time when we are just beginning to reacquaint ourselves with our emotions, patterns, scripts, needs, personal qualities, likes, and dislikes. In the active phase of our relationship addiction, we may not have known, or may have given up, our true selves, adapting like chameleons to someone else's likes and values, hoping that our adaptability would buy us love and security.

This focus inward in early recovery makes some people uncomfortable, given the negative connotations of the world *selfish.* Yet there is an important difference between the selfishness of someone who is self-centered and interested only in herself or himself—often at the expense of others—and the "self-ful," insightful, nurturing journey within of someone in early recovery. The psychologist Abraham Maslow studied a number of historical figures and living individuals of stature who, he believed, had realized their potentialities to the fullest. He found that they shared sixteen distinguishing characteristics; one of them was that they were problem-centered rather than self-centered. (A list of the sixteen characteristics of Maslow's self-actualizing people is reproduced in Appendix 12.)

At the core of the active phase of addictions is a disturbance of the self—a loss of the true self, which often gives way to a grandiose false self, capable of perceiving reality only from its own center, for its own interest. Problem-centered individuals, on the other hand, assess each situation prejudgment, acting on what seems best at that moment in time for all involved. Their decisions are based on what in Eastern thought would be called dharma—acting in attunement with the universal laws of reality.

Although at times we may pretend we don't need anyone, it is also a universal truth that humans are relational beings. To lead healthy lives that help us heal the past, we need others in our lives to grow with, to find expression for our love and empathy, and to nurture and be nurtured in return. People prone to addictive dependencies on others cannot isolate themselves from relationships any more than compulsive overeaters can forswear food. But just as overeaters can learn to recognize "irresistible" foods that trigger their compulsion, so relationship addicts *can* learn to identify types of partners likely to trigger "irresistible" dependencies.

Everyone has some dependencies; we are all interdependent. What distinguishes people with unhealthy dependencies from others is how they, as adults, respond when their dependency needs are not met. Relationship addicts need to discriminate between the human need for others and unhealthy neediness, so they can learn to love with detachment. (For a list of distinguishing characteristics of intimate versus addictive relationship behaviors, see Appendix 13.)

LOVE WITH DETACHMENT

The idea of love with detachment may be difficult to accept at first. The two terms seem mutually exclusive, yet it is the resolution of this paradox that lies at the heart of healing relationships. *Detachment* means neither aloofness, disinterest, nor disconnection. It is pointed out in Twelve-Step programs that *H*onesty, *O*penness, and *W*illingness are the "HOW" of recovery.

Detachment means seeing reality as it is, not as your dreams would like it to be. It means letting go of rigidly held plans, assumptions, and expectations. Finally, it means disentangling your personal boundaries from those of another person, getting a clearer sense of where your limits are or need to be. This is one way to stop using others as narcissistic extensions of yourself, and to recognize when you are being used by others in this way. Healing relationships, love, and personal transformation take place at that meeting point between the clearly defined *I* and *Thou*—which is also where a strong *We* has a chance to grow.

THE PERSONAL EXPANSION OF RECOVERY

Chapter 1 used the metaphor of the spiral as one way to understand the expansion of recovery that follows the contraction of addiction. But personal growth and transformation are not always a simple, upward, ever-expanding progression.

The day-by-day experience of recovery is more commonly that of someone hiking up a mountain: the path is narrow, uphill, and often riddled with rough terrain, detours, and unmarked intersections. Yet the hiker chooses to be there and at every moment chooses to keep moving forward, eyes focused on the step just ahead. The reward is in the footwork. So it is with the work of recovery: the possibilities it offers for improving relationships, vision, and personal transformation are the incentive.

The upward spiral of recovery is not a mirror image or exact reversal of the contraction spiral of addiction. *In our lives we are faced with a set of core issues that resurface again and again in different settings, with different people, at different times. These issues involve our relationship with the world, with ourselves, with our higher power. These are our life lessons.* When we are stuck, we may indeed go around in circles. But when we are engaged in the dynamic spiral of recovery, we deal with those issues on a different level than we did before. This is the process of transformation.

REBUILDING RELATIONSHIPS

Recovery from an unhealthy dependency can take place within the structure of an existing relationship. A new and patiently built relationship may emerge out of the genuine mutual love that was latently present. But changing the existing, entrenched dynamics of a formerly addictive relationship can be difficult for partners who want to stay together after one of them moves into recovery. During the active phase of an addiction, a relationship addict commonly cocreates an unbalanced partnership in which she is the chaser and her partner the distancer, or in which she assumes a "one-down" role in a subordinate/ dominant or learner/mentor relationship. Through the unconscious process of projective identification, she then disowns and abdicates her own strength and power, which are assumed, more or less willingly, by her partner.

In such a relationship, attempting to reestablish a latent deep connection that may still exist between the two partners is usually not enough. An unbalanced relationship usually requires the dismantling of the very structure of relationship, replacing it with a new order. Even though the recovering partner may now want a balanced peer relationship, she may find it difficult not to slip into old familiar roles. Her mate, despite the best of intentions, may not like having to relinquish the control and power of the existing structure. According to systems theory, one of his or her first moves may be to sabotage the efforts of the recovering partner in a more or less conscious attempt to reestablish the status quo.

The relationship addict in early recovery struggles to regain power from a one-down position, but may find that such a relationship must end in separation. Unable to affect the unyielding system, in frustration one or the other may solve the impasse by stepping out of the now unworkable arrangement. Sometimes the recovering relationship addict finds out that her former partner is now in the kind of well-balanced relationship they had unsuccessfully struggled to achieve. This may be annoying and mystifying, and she may ask herself, as many ex-lovers do, "Why is it that he is so willing to have with *her* the kind of relationship I begged for and he wouldn't hear of with *me*? Why couldn't he be like that when *we* were together?" The answer is that sometimes it is easier to create a new relationship more consonant to your current needs than it is to rebuild one based on premises that are no longer useful. But addictive relationships can be transformed when both partners are willing to make the internal changes that are usually needed in addition to external ones. Such changes have the best chance of succeeding under the guidance of a psychotherapist familiar with addictions and the dynamics of change.[2]

ENDINGS AND NEW BEGINNINGS

Not all couples wish to experience recovery together. Once a relationship addict stops contributing more than her share of energy toward keeping the partnership afloat, the lack of reciprocal commitment and caring may become apparent and the relationship may end. Or so many emotional wounds may have been mutually inflicted as to make a new start impossible. In some cases couples may also be unaware of what is required in recovery; they may lack the information, the resources, or the skills to change.

Recovery from relationship addiction sometimes begins with the ending of a difficult, emotionally painful relationship. It is at this point that some relationship addicts become determined not to repeat history. There is a certain advantage to this timing; when the decision to change coincides with the ending of a relationship, early recovery can unfold naturally, without the confounding stresses of partnership.

Having your own emotional space at such a time has value. It gives you time to make sense of the past, to grieve opportunities missed, promises broken, dreams lost, and to experience the keenly felt sense of failure that often follows the breakup of a significant love relationship.

In our culture we support grief for the loss of a loved one through death, yet—even though the grieving process is the same—we often show little compassion for or patience with others, and even less with ourselves, for the slow, natural, and essential evolution of grief at the end of relationships. The initial denial, the gradual awakening to reality, the intense grief, the slow process of letting go, the forgiveness, the making emotional closure on the relationship must all take place whether we grieve a death or the end of a close relationship. Only by honoring our memories and grief can we learn the final lessons of relationships that needed to end, so that we may avoid repeating those same mistakes in the future. Only in forgiving, in letting go of past blame, can we ward off the corrosive effect on ourselves and others of anger, grudges, and resentments. And only with a farewell in which we give a blessing and ask to receive the blessing of the other can we go through the final phase of the grief process: getting on with our separate lives, leaving no unfinished business behind us to haunt our future hopes and loves.

SPIRITUALITY

Relationship addiction—as with all unhealthy dependencies—is an attempt to heal our perceived deficits through something outside ourselves, when in reality our inner sense of emptiness is a spiritual void. It is for this reason that many themes from the spiritual tradition have been woven into this book. Introspection, an openness to what is, a willingness to take responsibility for our choices, to "let go," to surrender, to acknowledge that what we want is not always what we need, and the idea that intimacy with others can take place only through intimacy with ourselves—these are all means by which we can begin turning our focus inward. Spirit has the capacity to fill the inner void in a lasting way that heals the wounds of our souls and nourishes our human striving for self-transformation.

In contrast to religion—the way in which human beings attempt to systematize belief in a higher power through specific definitions of that power, and through rituals, rules of conduct, and philosophical frameworks—spirituality is an individual, subjective expression of awe and reverence for something greater than oneself. There are many spiritual paths; authentic paths are all founded on the same set of universal truths, and all lead to truth and spiritual enlightenment. They share the same seven stages of unfolding for those who seek transformation:[3]

1. surrender
2. purification
3. right relationship with self and others
4. living in the here and now
5. the dawning of understanding

6. living and loving wisely
7. authentic being

It is this spiritual tradition that distinguishes Twelve-Step programs from other therapy and support groups, and accounts for their success in helping people overcome their addictions. Psychotherapy groups focus on personality and work with the material and interactions produced by the group members; Twelve-Step groups are grounded in a set of spiritual principles by which to live. Therapy groups' underlying goals include helping members to develop self-awareness so they may improve their interpersonal skills and relationships; Twelve-Step programs offer their members a set of broad universal values that support and guide them no matter what situation they encounter. (The Twelve Steps of Alcoholics Anonymous are reproduced in Appendix 14.) Religious groups are also founded on values, but unlike Twelve-Step groups they require their followers to share a common understanding of God and certain prescribed behaviors. Twelve-Step groups, on the other hand, encourage individual definitions of God or Higher Power and leave the "how to's" of the spiritual journey to each individual's own way of weaving the twelve steps into his or her life.

For some it is difficult to distinguish between the spiritual belief in a Higher Power and the God of their childhood. But because the Twelve-Step philosophy does not impose a specific view of a Higher Power, for some a Higher Power may be God, Christ, another divine entity, a prophet, or a spiritual guide. For others it may be the power of the ocean or of the group.

What is important is the willingness to acknowledge that there is something greater than yourself, that you don't know everything, that you don't have a master plan, that you are not in control of events and other people. Spirituality is much more than the worship of and reverence toward an external divinity. It acknowledges and does homage to the spark of divinity within each of us; it is an approach to life, a point of view, an attitude. It is a surrender to the belief in a greater purpose, a greater plan and wisdom than your own. It is a trust that things will unfold as they must if you just do the footwork, staying attuned to your inner guidance, putting forth the effort, letting go of attachment to the results, and believing in divine guidance and the choices it offers.

Spirituality must be lived, practiced consistently, and acted on consciously. A person's spirituality is only partly revealed by words and actions. Because the spiritual path is a commitment to personal transformation, to service, and to not harming others, it manifests most clearly in a person's attitude toward life, toward others, and toward the self. The spiritual path is a blend of intent and openness to our intuition and unconscious motives, a willingness to trust, a willingness to be tolerant and gentle, a willingness to keep learning from life's lessons. It is an attunement to what is called for at each moment, on each occasion. Spiritual attunement has less to do with action than with a conscious choice to surrender to the spontaneous unfolding of what is, as illustrated by the Taoist concept of *wu-wei*.

Thus *wu-wei* as "not forcing" is what we mean by going with the grain, rolling with the punch, swimming with the current, trimming sails to the wind, taking the tide at its flood, and stooping to conquer. . . .
The principle is illustrated by the parable of the pine and the willow in heavy snow. The pine branch, being rigid, cracks under the weight; but the willow branch [being springy] yields to the weight, and the snow drops off. *Wu-wei* . . . must be understood primarily as a form of intelligence—that is, of knowing the principles, structures, and trends of human and natural affairs so well that one uses the least amount of energy in dealing with them.[1]

Spiritual practices are the means for enhancing this attunement, this "not forcing." Spiritual practices, such as meditation, chanting, praying, attendance at Twelve-Step meetings and applications of these principles in your life, journal writing, service to the community, and openness and gentleness in your relationships, can all be satisfying ways to get in touch with your inner voice, and often are a way to start feeling again a long lost sense of joy and gratitude in the everyday activities and encounters of your life.

When we first choose to travel the path of personal transformation rather than the one of self-seeking or self-gratification, the shift in our perceptions begins to affect the way we filter information, how we work and what we choose to work on, and how we relate to others and with whom we choose to relate. In short, we construct an entirely new framework for what is useful and what is useless in our lives, making our decisions accordingly. In order to become more congruent with who we are becoming, we may first have to let go of many structures and dreams we had built. Likewise, we may choose to stay in relationships or situations that formerly seemed without value, because we know they have something to teach us.

This period of letting go may be painful, but we can accept it because we have learned the difference between hurtful and harmful. The hurt of letting go is often nothing more than the gap between reality and fantasy. Yet now we recognize the difference between this hurt and the harm that we experience when we surrender our inner core. We learn that nothing can harm us except this surrender of self and our own interpretations and attitudes. We play fewer and fewer games, and place blame less often. We step back from situations, let things take their natural course, strive to live an unscripted life. Perhaps more important, we release others. The poet Rainer Maria Rilke's definition of love, "Love consists in this, that two solitudes protect and touch and greet one another" is so poignant because the word *solitudes* encompasses the essence of human dilemma: we are relational beings, yet each of us is ultimately alone. And so at times both the path to relationship and the path to self-transformation are traveled alone. Intimacy with self is the compass that guides the way.

> We are going to know a new freedom and a new happiness.
> We will not regret the past or wish to shut the door on it.
> We will comprehend the word serenity and we will know peace.
> No matter how far down the scale we have gone, we will see how our experience can benefit others.
> That feeling of uselessness and self-pity will disappear.
> We will lose interest in selfish things and gain interest in our fellows.
> Self-seeking will slip away.
> Our whole attitude and outlook upon life will change.
> Fear of people and of economic insecurity will leave us.
> We will intuitively know how to handle situations which used to baffle us.
> We will suddenly realize that God is doing for us what we could not do for ourselves.[5]

Johnson's Feeling Chart

The following is the authors' adaptation of the Feeling Chart, developed by Dr. Vernon Johnson, founder of the Johnson Institute in Minneapolis, which describes a four-stage evolution of alcohol addiction. Other addictions, such as overeating, relationship dependence, and drug abuse, can also be viewed in this way.

1. *Experiencing* the mood swing brought about by the addictive substance: at this early stage the swing is in a positive direction and is pleasant. Drinkers experiment with dosage, learning to control the degree of the mood swing in this way.
2. *Seeking* the mood swing, looking forward to it, anticipating it: the behavior becomes directed toward experiencing euphoria. At this stage drinkers typically start watching the clock, waiting for the cocktail hour, for Friday night's party, for the business lunch, and so on. Some mood swing experiences begin to be physically negative. Hangovers, confusion, embarrassment at later reports of their behavior become more common. But to drinkers the fun had while intoxicated was well worth it. Because the swing back to normal can still be made, they are not paying a significant emotional price for the drinking yet.
3. *Harmful dependence:* it is at this stage that drinkers cross over that invisible line between abuse and dependence (or attachment and addiction). Drinking for pleasure, for the fun of the mood swing, is no longer primary. Much of the time they drink just to relieve stress. The emotional cost of their drinking is increasingly great. When they swing back, often they are unable to make it back to normal—they are in pain. They have lost control—yet they are unaware that they are in trouble.

   Typical indicators of harmful dependence include obsession (thoughts are constantly directed toward the addictive substance), compulsion (most of the time behavior is directed toward the addictive substance), tolerance increase (needing more of the substance to obtain the same effect), which is often followed by tolerance decrease (some alcoholics are suddenly no longer able to drink as much as they used to), anxious protection of the supply (standing close to the bar, undue anxiety about running out of a favorite drink at home, and so on), and withdrawal (physical symptoms, such as sweating, trembling, anxiety, panic appear when the supply is not available).

4. *Drinking to feel normal:* in this fourth and final stage of alcoholism, drinkers are no longer able to start their drinking from a point of normal, because they are in a state of chronic emotional pain and depression. The behavior originally aimed at feeling euphoric no longer provides a high. At this stage alcoholics drink just to feel normal, but instead drinking merely worsens their emotional state. Their lives are in shambles. They lie to cover up their blackouts and their problems from friends and employers. Their feelings of free-floating anxiety, shame, and guilt only make things worse.

Symptoms of Alcoholism

	YES	NO

1. PREOCCUPATION

    A. Do you ever look forward to the end of a day's work so that you can have a couple of drinks and relax?   ____ ____

    B. Do you sometimes look forward to the end of the week so that you can have some fun drinking?   ____ ____

    C. Does the thought of drinking sometimes enter your mind when you should be thinking of something else?   ____ ____

    D. Do you sometimes feel the need to have a drink at a particular time of the day?   ____ ____

2. GULPING DRINKS

    A. Do you usually order a double or like to have your first two or three drinks quickly?   ____ ____

    B. Do you sometimes have a couple of drinks before going to a party or out to dinner?   ____ ____

3. INCREASED TOLERANCE

    A. Do you find that you can often drink more than others and not show it too much?   ____ ____

    B. Has anyone ever commented on your ability to hold your liquor?   ____ ____

    C. Have you ever wondered about your increased capacity to drink and perhaps felt somewhat proud of it?   ____ ____

4. USE OF ALCOHOL AS A MEDICINE

    A. Do you ever drink to calm your nerves or reduce tension?   ____ ____

    B. Do you find it difficult to enjoy a party or dance if there is nothing to drink?   ____ ____

C. Do you ever use alcohol as a nightcap to help you get to sleep at night? ___ ___

D. Do you ever use alcohol to relieve physical discomfort? ___ ___

5. DRINKING ALONE

A. Do you ever stop in a bar and have a couple of drinks by yourself? ___ ___

B. Do you sometimes drink at home alone or when no one else is drinking? ___ ___

6. BLACKOUT

A. In the morning after an evening of drinking, have you ever had the experience of not being able to remember everything that happened on the night before? ___ ___

B. Have you ever had difficulty recalling how you got home after a night's drinking? ___ ___

7. SECLUDED BOTTLE

A. Do you sometimes hide a bottle in the house in the event you may need a drink sometime? ___ ___

B. Do you ever keep a bottle in the trunk or your car just in case you may need a drink? ___ ___

8. NONPREMEDITATED DRINKING

A. Do you ever stop in to have two or three drinks and have several more than you planned? ___ ___

B. Do you ever find yourself stopping in for a drink when you planned to go straight home or someplace else? ___ ___

C. Are you sometimes one of the last ones to leave a bar or a drinking party when you had planned to go home earlier in the evening? ___ ___

D. Do you sometimes drink more than you think you should? ___ ___

E. Is your drinking sometimes different from what you would like it to be? ___ ___

9. MORNING TREMORS

A. Have you ever had the shakes or tremors of the hands after a night of drinking? ___ ___

10. MORNING DRINK

A. Have you ever taken a drink in the morning to help you over a hangover? ___ ___

How many of these questions did you answer Yes? ___

No one can settle for you the question of whether or not you are an alcoholic. If you answered even one question Yes, you will want to watch yourself. If you answered three or more Yes, or if you can notice a drift in the affirmative, you have a definite reason to worry.

Source: Women's Alcoholism Center, San Francisco, California.

Am I a Food Addict?

	YES	NO
1. Do you get hungry when things are not going your way?	___	___
2. Do you get hungry when there doesn't seem to be anything to do?	___	___
3. After you have been frightened or scared about something that has happened, do you find yourself hungry?	___	___
4. When you feel "all alone" do you sometimes use food to get over the feeling?	___	___
5. After an argument with someone do you find yourself wanting to eat?	___	___
6. Have you ever found yourself eating two breakfasts, lunches, or dinners because you felt the first one was inadequate?	___	___
7. Do you find yourself planning the next meal before you've finished eating?	___	___
8. When you sit down to a meal do you find you eat more than you want to?	___	___
9. Do you ever have a sense of being out of control during a meal?	___	___
10. Have you ever sought outside help to deal with your eating?	___	___
11. Do you feel "fat" or "obese"?	___	___
12. Do you fear becoming fat or larger than present?	___	___
13. Have you attempted any of the following methods to control your weight?	___	___
Strict dieting	___	___
Self-Induced Vomiting	___	___
Laxatives	___	___

Diuretics   — —
Diet Pills   — —
Vigorous Exercise — —
Fasting   — —

Source: The Rader Institute, San Diego, California.

Prescription Pill Dependence

	YES	NO

1. Are there times you use an extra dose to get through a tough situation? ___ ___
2. Do you need an extra dose now and then to calm down? Then, after the tough situation is over, do you take an extra dose? ___ ___
3. Has your dosage increased over time? ___ ___
4. Have you used your prescription for three or more years? ___ ___
5. When you miss taking your usual dose do you become depressed, shaky, or nervous? ___ ___
6. Do you now take something in addition to your prescription to get relief? ___ ___
7. Do you now take your prescription to help with problems which are different from the one you originally needed it for? ___ ___
8. Are you agitated even after you have taken your usual dosage? ___ ___
9. Are you occasionally disoriented or have mental lapses? ___ ___
10. Did you get your prescription for occasional use, but now use it regularly? ___ ___
11. Do you find yourself increasingly forgetful or irritated by minor upsets? ___ ___
12. Have you gotten upset when a refill was refused? ___ ___
13. Has your doctor suggested that you reduce the amount you are taking? ___ ___
14. Are you receiving prescriptions from more than one doctor or at more than one pharmacy? ___ ___
15. Do you ask for your prescription at each doctor's visit? ___ ___
16. Do you minimize the amount you take to your family, friends, or physician? ___ ___
17. Do you spend any time justifying your need for increased medicine? ___ ___

18. Do you find yourself drinking when you are out of   ___ ___
    your prescription?
19. Have you tried to quit or cut down on your own and   ___ ___
    found it impossible? (It is unsafe to abruptly stop any
    psychoactive drug without medical supervision.)
20. Do you find yourself checking out other people's   ___ ___
    medicine cabinets or taking other people's pills?

Source: Community Resources and Self-Help, San Diego, CA. Reprinted with permission.

Drug Addiction

<table>
<thead>
<tr><th></th><th>YES</th><th>NO</th></tr>
</thead>
<tbody>
<tr><td>1. Do you avoid people and and/or places that do not condone your usage?</td><td>___</td><td>___</td></tr>
<tr><td>2. Do you spend your money on drugs rather than food and other necessities?</td><td>___</td><td>___</td></tr>
<tr><td>3. Do you think that everyone in the world is crazy except yourself?</td><td>___</td><td>___</td></tr>
<tr><td>4. Do you wonder why some people don't want to use?</td><td>___</td><td>___</td></tr>
<tr><td>5. Does the thought of running out of drugs leave you with a feeling of impending doom?</td><td>___</td><td>___</td></tr>
<tr><td>6. Do you guard your supply?</td><td>___</td><td>___</td></tr>
<tr><td>7. Do you get more drugs when your supply is running low or as soon as you run out?</td><td>___</td><td>___</td></tr>
<tr><td>8. Do you like to use alone?</td><td>___</td><td>___</td></tr>
<tr><td>9. Have you tried substituting one drug for another, thinking that "one" particular drug was your problem?</td><td>___</td><td>___</td></tr>
<tr><td>10. Do you neglect your responsibilities because you'd rather get high?</td><td>___</td><td>___</td></tr>
<tr><td>11. Do you use because your family drives you crazy?</td><td>___</td><td>___</td></tr>
<tr><td>12. Do you con doctors for "legal" drugs, telling yourself that it's okay to use them because they aren't illegal?</td><td>___</td><td>___</td></tr>
<tr><td>13. Do you have more than one prescription at one time with different doctors?</td><td>___</td><td>___</td></tr>
<tr><td>14. Do you use something to help you get going in the morning, or to slow you down at night?</td><td>___</td><td>___</td></tr>
<tr><td>15. Do you use illegal or "hard" drugs and think there is nothing that can be done to kick the habit?</td><td>___</td><td>___</td></tr>
<tr><td>16. Have you ever been in trouble with friends, family, school, jobs or the law because of drug-related incidents?</td><td>___</td><td>___</td></tr>
<tr><td>17. Have you been arrested for drinking or drunk driving?</td><td>___</td><td>___</td></tr>
<tr><td>18. Do you steal drugs or money to buy drugs?</td><td>___</td><td>___</td></tr>
</tbody>
</table>

19. Do you have more than one hiding place for your drugs? ___ ___

20. Do you have empty alcohol containers in your vehicle? ___ ___

21. Did you smoke your plant before it was two feet tall? ___ ___

22. Do you steal your friend's drugs? ___ ___

23. Do you fight over the cotton shot, or the biggest line? ___ ___

24. Have you ever shot or snorted your best friend's morning (wake-up) high? ___ ___

25. Have you ever sharpened a needle on a match box? ___ ___

26. Do you collect paraphernalia? ___ ___

27. Do you take drugs that you don't prefer? ___ ___

28. Do you do things while under the influence that you would not do while straight? ___ ___

29. Do you hide your drugs, even if you live alone? ___ ___

30. Have the good times gone from your using? ___ ___

31. Have you searched other people's medicine cabinets? ___ ___

32. Do you think you must be high to have a good time? ___ ___

33. Do you ever question your own sanity? ___ ___

34. Do you lie about what or how much you use? ___ ___

35. Do you use drugs to overcome your fear of people? ___ ___

36. Have you considered suicide? ___ ___

37. Are you preoccupied with getting high? ___ ___

38. Have you tried to control your using? ___ ___

39. Do all of your activities center around drugs? ___ ___

40. Are you ashamed of your using? ___ ___

41. Have you ever over-dosed? ___ ___

42. Have you ever tried to quit and failed? ___ ___

43. Do you choose your friends by the drugs they have? ___ ___

44. Do you think you might have a drug problem? ___ ___

45. Do you want to stop using, but can't do it alone? ___ ___

Source: *Am I an Addict?*, 1983, Van Nuys, CA: World Service Office, Inc., Narcotics Anonymous.

Did You Grow Up With A Problem Drinker. . . .

	YES	NO
1. Do you constantly seek approval and affirmation?	___	___
2. Do you fail to recognize your accomplishments?	___	___
3. Do you fear criticism?	___	___
4. Do you overextend yourself?	___	___
5. Have you had problems with your own compulsive behavior?	___	___
6. Do you have a need for perfection?	___	___
7. Are you uneasy when your life is going smoothly, continually anticipating problems?	___	___
8. Do you feel more alive in the midst of a crisis?	___	___
9. Do you feel responsible for others, as you did for the problem drinker in your life?	___	___
10. Do you care for others easily, yet find it difficult to care for yourself?	___	___
11. Do you isolate yourself from other people?	___	___
12. Do you respond with anxiety to authority figures and angry people?	___	___
13. Do you feel that individuals and society in general are taking advantage of you?	___	___
14. Do you have trouble with intimate relationships?	___	___
15. Do you confuse pity with love, as you did with the problem drinker?	___	___
16. Do you attract and seek people who tend to be compulsive?	___	___
17. Do you cling to relationships because you are afraid of being alone?	___	___
18. Do you often mistrust your own feelings and the feelings expressed by others?	___	___

19. Do you find it difficult to express your emotions? ___ ___
20. Do you think parental drinking may have affected ___ ___
   you?

Compulsive Gambling

	YES	NO
1. Did you ever lose time from work due to gambling?	___	___
2. Has gambling ever made your home life unhappy?	___	___
3. Did gambling affect your reputation?	___	___
4. Have you ever felt remorse after gambling?	___	___
5. Did you ever gamble to get money with which to pay debts or otherwise solve financial difficulties?	___	___
6. Did gambling cause a decrease in your ambition or efficiency?	___	___
7. After losing did you feel you must return as soon as possible and win back your losses?	___	___
8. After a win did you have a strong urge to return and win more?	___	___
9. Did you often gamble until your last dollar was gone?	___	___
10. Did you ever borrow to finance your gambling?	___	___
11. Have you ever sold anything to finance your gambling?	___	___
12. Were you reluctant to use "gambling money" for normal expenditures?	___	___
13. Did gambling make you careless of the welfare of your family?	___	___
14. Did you ever gamble longer than you had planned?	___	___
15. Have you ever gambled to escape worry or trouble?	___	___
16. Have you ever committed, or considered committing, an illegal act to finance gambling?	___	___
17. Did gambling cause you to have difficulty in sleeping?	___	___
18. Do arguments, disappointments or frustrations create within you an urge to gamble?	___	___
19. Did you ever have an urge to celebrate any good fortune by a few hours of gambling?	___	___
20. Have you ever considered self-destruction as a result of your gambling?	___	___

Source: The Twelve-Step Program of Gamblers Anonymous. Reprinted with permission.

Sexual Addiction

	YES	NO

1. Have you ever thought you needed help for your sexual thinking or behavior?
2. That you'd be better off if you didn't keep "giving in"?
3. That sex or stimuli are controlling you?
4. Have you ever tried to stop or limit doing what you felt was wrong in your sexual behavior?
5. Do you resort to sex to escape, relieve anxiety, or because you can't cope?
6. Do you feel guilt, remorse or depression afterward?
7. Has your pursuit of sex become more compulsive?
8. Does it interfere with relations with your spouse?
9. Do you have to resort to images or memories during sex?
10. Does an irresistible impulse arise when the other party makes the overtures or sex is offered?
11. Do you keep going from one "relationship" or lover to another?
12. Do you feel the "right relationship" would help you stop lusting, masturbating, or being so promiscuous?
13. Do you have a destructive need—a desperate sexual or emotional need for someone?
14. Does pursuit of sex make you careless for yourself or the welfare of your family or others?
15. Has your effectiveness or concentration decreased as sex has become more compulsive?
16. Do you lose time from work for it?
17. Do you turn to a lower environment when pursuing sex?
18. Do you want to get away from the sex partner as soon as possible after the act?

19. Although your spouse is sexually compatible, do you still masturbate or have sex with others?   ___ ___

20. Have you ever been arrested for a sex-related offense?   ___ ___

Source: Sexaholics Anonymous. Copyright © 1985 by SA Literature. Reprinted by permission.

Relationship Addiction

	YES	NO

1. Typically, you come from a dysfunctional home in which your emotional needs were not met. ____ ____
2. Having received little real nurturing yourself, you try to fill this unmet need vicariously by becoming a care-giver, especially to men who appear, in some way, needy. ____ ____
3. Because you were never able to change your parent(s) into the warm, loving caretaker(s) you longed for, you respond deeply to the familiar type of emotionally unavailable man whom you can again try to change, through your love. ____ ____
4. Terrified of abandonment, you will do anything to keep a relationship from dissolving. ____ ____
5. Almost nothing is too much trouble, takes too much time, or is too expensive if it will "help" the man you are involved with. ____ ____
6. Accustomed to lack of love in personal relationships, you are willing to wait, hope, and try harder to please. ____ ____
7. You are willing to take far more than 50 percent of the responsibility, guilt, and blame in any relationship. ____ ____
8. Your self-esteem is critically low, and deep inside you do not believe you deserve to be happy. Rather, you believe you must earn the right to enjoy life. ____ ____
9. You have a desperate need to control your men and your relationships, having experienced little security in childhood. You mask your efforts to control people and situations as "being helpful." ____ ____
10. In a relationship, you are much more in touch with your dream of how it could be than with the reality of your situation. ____ ____
11. You are addicted to men and to emotional pain. ____ ____

12. You may be predisposed emotionally and often bio-chemically to becoming addicted to drugs, alcohol, and/or certain foods, particularly sugary ones. ___ ___

13. By being drawn to people with problems that need fixing, or by being enmeshed in situations that are chaotic, uncertain, and emotionally painful, you avoid focusing on your responsibility to yourself. ___ ___

14. You may have a tendency toward episodes of depression, which you try to forestall through the excitement provided by an unstable relationship. ___ ___

15. You are not attracted to men who are kind, stable, reliable, and interested in you. You find such "nice" men boring. ___ ___

Source: Robin Norwood, *Women Who Love Too Much* (Los Angeles: Tarcher, 1985), 10–11. Reprinted with permission.

Warning Signs of Addictive Behavior

1. Saying or doing something dishonest—even the slightest kind of lie counts.
2. Talking about the significant other in a way you wouldn't do if he or she were present, usually to build up allies and justify yourself.
3. Catching yourself obsessing about the significant other or a situation; doing "what ifs" or "if onlys."
4. Noticing your inclination to control or be manipulative.
5. Starting to interpret a significant other and assuming you know more about that person than he or she does about himself or herself.
6. Self-neglect.
7. Comparisons. The process of comparing oneself with others is addictive in itself. Statements such as, "I cannot do it as well" or "If only I could be like her" are danger signals.
8. Jealousy. Jealousy is an expression of the relationship addict's "protection of the supply."
9. All-or-nothing thinking (black/white, good/bad, right/wrong, either/or).
10. Add your own:

Source: Adapted from Anne Wilson Schaef, *Co-dependence: Misunderstood–Mistreated* (San Francisco: Harper & Row, 1986).

Kinsey's Heterosexual–Homosexual Rating Scale

0 Exclusively heterosexual
1 Predominantly heterosexual; only incidentally homosexual
2 Predominantly heterosexual; more than incidentally homosexual
3 Equally heterosexual and homosexual
4 Predominantly homosexual; more than incidentally heterosexual
5 Predominantly homosexual; only incidentally heterosexual
6 Exclusively homosexual

Source: Adapted from A. C. Kinsey, W. B. Pomeroy, and C. E. Martin, *Sexual Behavior in the Human Male* (Philadelphia: Saunders, 1948). Reprinted by permission of the Kinsey Institute for Research in Sex, Gender, and Reproduction, Inc.

Sixteen Distinguishing Features of Self-Actualizing People by Abraham Maslow

Humanist psychologist Abraham Maslow made an intensive and far-reaching investigation of a group of self-actualizing people. His sample included historical figures, such as Lincoln, Jefferson, Walt Whitman, Thoreau, and Beethoven. Others, such as Eleanor Roosevelt and Einstein, were living at the time of Maslow's investigation.

Maslow found that self-actualizing people share the following qualities:

1. They are realistically oriented;
2. They accept themselves, other people, and the natural world for what they are;
3. They have a great deal of spontaneity;
4. They are problem-centered rather than self-centered;
5. They have an air of detachment and a need for privacy;
6. They are autonomous and independent;
7. Their appreciation of people and things is fresh rather than stereotyped;
8. Most of them have had profound mystical or spiritual experiences, although not necessarily religious in character;
9. They identify with mankind;
10. Their intimate relationships with a few specially loved people tend to be profound and deeply emotional rather than superficial;
11. Their values and attitudes are democratic;
12. They do not confuse means with ends;
13. Their sense of humor is philosophical rather than hostile;
14. They have a great fund of creativeness;
15. They resist conformity to the culture;
16. They transcend the environment rather than just coping with it.

Source: Calvin S. Hall and Gardner Lindzey, *Theories of Personality*, third ed. (New York: John Wiley & Sons, 1978), pp. 269–70. Reprinted with permission.

Relationships—Intimate versus Addictive

Intimacy	*Addiction*
Peers.	Power differential.
Mutuality.	Imbalance.
Choice.	Loss of choice.
Freedom.	Compulsion.
Desire to share needs and feelings.	No-talk rule, especially if things are not working out.
Relationship always changing.	Relationship always the same.
I *want* to be there.	I *have* to be there.
I begin with me (self). I want. . . . I feel. . . . Initiator.	I begin with you. *You* change. You make me feel. . . . Reactor, responder.
I take care of me. I am solely responsible for figuring out what I need and for communicating it to you.	You will know what's right for me and you will fix it.
Relationship deals with reality.	Relationship is based on delusion.
Relationship deals with things as they are, whatever comes along.	Relationship uses denial and avoidance to deal with things.
My dedication to you is based on my true interest in your spiritual path, even if it takes you away.	Your spiritual growth doesn't count.
Love is always an act of self-love.	Love is wanting someone to love me at all costs.

The addiction process in a relationship follows the same pattern as chemical dependence:

Tolerance increase—Requires more and more to get the same effect.

Obsessive thoughts—Mental preoccupation with the object of addiction.

Compulsive behavior—Inflexibility and rigidity of behavior.

Protecting the supply—Possessiveness.

Withdrawal symptoms—Acute discomfort at any separation from object of addiction.

The addicted person looks for something outside herself or himself to feel whole.

It is important to distinguish between *needy* (looking for someone to make you whole) and *needing* (wanting someone important in your life who is not necessary for your survival).

Source: Stephanie S. Covington, Ph.D.

The Twelve Steps of Alcoholics Anonymous

1. We admitted we were powerless over alcohol—that our lives had become unmanageable.
2. Came to believe that a Power greater than ourselves could restore us to sanity.
3. Made a decision to turn our will and our lives over to the care of God as we understood Him.
4. Made a searching and fearless moral inventory of ourselves.
5. Admitted to God, to ourselves and to another human being the exact nature of our wrongs.
6. Were entirely ready to have God remove all these defects of character.
7. Humbly asked Him to remove our shortcomings.
8. Made a list of all persons we had harmed and became willing to make amends to them all.
9. Made direct amends to such people wherever possible except when to do so would injure them or others.
10. Continued to take personal inventory and when we were wrong promptly admitted it.
11. Sought through prayer and meditation to improve our conscious contact with God as we understood Him, praying only for knowledge of His will for us and the power to carry that out.
12. Having had a spiritual awakening as the result of these Steps, we tried to carry this message to others, and to practice these principles in all our affairs.

Source: The Twelve Steps reprinted with permission of Alcoholics Anonymous World Services, Inc.

Note: The first step is often adapted by other Twelve-Step groups for other addictions such as food, sex, drugs, other people, etc.

Notes

PROLOGUE

1. All quotations in this prologue are from Robert Johnson's *We: Understanding the Psychology of Romantic Love,* (San Francisco: Harper & Row, 1983).

CHAPTER 1

1. The emotional process described here and in the diagram in figure 1 is adapted from a model of the emotional evolution of alcohol addiction developed by Vernon E. Johnson, as described in *I'll Quit Tomorrow* (San Francisco: Harper & Row, 1980). (See Appendix 1 for more information.)
2. The concept of the addiction spiral is adapted from Stephanie Brown's book *Treating the Alcoholic: A Developmental Model of Recovery* (New York: John Wiley & Sons, 1985), p. 49. The diagram in fig. 2 is from the same source.

CHAPTER 2

1. Similar family strengths have been identified by many family systems theorists and researchers. The six listed here are adapted from the studies of N. Stinette and J. Defrain of the University of Nebraska Research Center on Family Strengths and authors of *Secrets of Strong Families* (Boston: Little, Brown and Company, 1985), p. 48.
2. This explanation of family roles is from the book *Another Chance,* by Sharon Wegscheider, a pioneer in working with alcoholic family systems (pp. 55–56).
3. This is the point made by author Claudia Black, M.S.W., Ph.D., in her book about adult children of alcoholics, *It Will Never Happen to Me!* (Denver, Co: M.A.C., 1982), p. 4.
4. You may find valuable clues to your own heritage by developing your personal family tree, including the branches of current and former significant partners. Pay attention not only to the trail and pattern of dysfunctions and addictions, but also to the blanks, the areas about which you know nothing. Often those blank spots are where the family secrets are.
5. The term *father hunger* was originally coined by psychoanalyst J. Herzog to refer to the effects of a physically absent father. Based

on recent research, others (John Munder Ross, Samuel Osherson, and Andrew Merton) have expanded its definition to include psychologically absent fathers.

6. Excerpted from "Father Hunger," an article by Andrew Merton, in *New Age Journal*, September/October 1986, p. 26.

CHAPTER 3

1. Notably in *Your Inner Child of the Past*, by W. Hugh Missildine, M.D. (New York: Pocket Books, 1963) and in *Games People Play*, by Eric Berne, M.D. (New York: Ballantine Books, 1964).

2. In *Touching*, by Ashley Montagu, second edition (New York: Harper & Row, 1978), p. 79.

3. H. H. Harlow and R. R. Zimmerman, "The Development of Affectional Responses in Infant Monkeys," *Proceedings, American Philosophical Society* 102 (1958): 87.

4. Berne, *Games People Play*.

5. Jean Baker Miller, *Toward a New Psychology of Women*, second edition (Boston: Beacon Press, 1986).

6. Quoted in *In a Different Voice*, by Carol Gilligan (Cambridge: Harvard University Press, 1982).

7. Quoted from *Empathy and Self Boundaries*, by Judith V. Jordan, Ph.D., Work in Progress (Wellesley, MA: Stone Center for Developmental Services and Studies, no. 16, 1984), p. 6.

8. For a theoretical discussion of self-empathy, refer to Jordan, *Empathy and Self Boundaries*.

9. The term *being-in-relationship* and the interpretation of Erikson's first four stages of development summarized in this chapter were developed by Jean Baker Miller, M.D., *The Development of Women's Sense of Self*, Work in Progress (Wellesley, MA: Stone Center for Developmental Services and Studies, no. 12, 1984), pp. 2-4.

10. Janet Surrey, Ph.D., *Self-in-Relation: A Theory of Women's Development*, Work in Progress (Wellesley, MA: Stone Center for Developmental Services and Studies, no. 13, 1985), p. 8.

11. Quoted in "Treatment for Women: What Can We Do with What We Know?" in *Women and Addiction, A Collection of Papers*, by Stephanie Covington (La Jolla, CA: 1985).

12. This script inventory was adapted from one developed by Dawn Miller and Ralph Miller, Ph.D. Courtesy of the authors.

CHAPTER 4

1. The model and roles were developed by Sharon Wegscheider, a counselor with extensive experience working with alcoholic families; *Another Chance: Hope and Health for the Alcoholic Family* (Palo Alto, CA: Science and Behavior Books, 1981).

2. The situational leadership model was developed by Paul Hersey and Ken Blanchard, *Management of Organizational Behavior: Utilizing Human Resources,* fourth ed. (Englewood Cliffs, N.J.: Prentice-Hall, Inc., 1982).
3. The concept of the "good-enough" mother was developed by British object relations theorist D. W. Winnicott, "The Theory of the Parent-Infant Relationship," in *The Maturational Process and the Facilitating Environment* (New York: I.U.P., 1960).

CHAPTER 5

1. Paul Watzlawick, Ph.D., et al., *Change, Principles of Problem Formation and Problem Resolution* (New York: W. W. Norton, 1974).
2. Matthew McKay, et al., *Messages: The Communication Book* (Oakland, Calif.: New Harbinger Publications, 1983). p. 58.
3. Leo F. Buscaglia, *Loving Each Other: The Challenge of Human Relationships* (New York: Fawcett Columbine, 1984).
4. William J. Lederer and Don Jackson, M.D., *The Mirages of Marriage* (New York: W. W. Norton, 1968).
5. Watzlawick, *Change.*
6. Merle A. Fossum and Marilyn J. Mason, *Facing Shame: Families in Recovery* (New York: W. W. Norton, 1986), 71.
7. Kahlil Gibran, *The Prophet* (New York: Alfred A. Knopf, 1923).
8. This section was adapted from the relapse prevention studies of G. Alan Marlatt and his associates with alcoholics, smokers, and heroin addicts. G. Alan Marlatt and Judith R. Gordon, "Determinants of Relapse: Implications for the Maintenance of Behavior Change," in *Behavioral Medicine: Changing Health Lifestyles,* P. O. Davidson, Ph.D., and S. M. Davidson, M.S.N., ed. (New York: Brunner/Mazel, 1980).

CHAPTER 6

1. Dinah Maria Mulock Craik: "Friendship," in *Best Loved Poems of the American People,* Hazel Felleman (Garden City: Garden City Books, 1936), p. 43.
2. *The Ethics of Aristotle: The Nichomachean Ethics,* trans. J. A. K. Thomson (New York: Viking Penguin, 1953). p. 271.
3. Barbara Ehrenreich, "In Praise of 'Best Friends'," *Ms.,* January 1987. p. 35.
4. Annette Goodheart, Ph.D., *Laugh Your Way to Health: Laughter and Relationships.* (From an audiotape series by Dr. Annette Goodheart, 1985).
5. Merle Shain, *When Lovers Are Friends* (New York: Bantam Books, 1978). p. 65.
6. In mathematical equations, the equal sign balances the two unlike statements on either side of it, thereby declaring that although dif-

ferent, their values match. So it is with equality in personal relationships. Equality never implies sameness, only *equivalence*—equivalent value for different contributions.

In the past few years, the women's movement has reintroduced into prominence the term *equity,* which derives from the same Latin root as *equality* (that is, *aequus,* or even). In English, *equity* has connotations of fairness and justice. Therefore it is the most appropriate word in debating the just remuneration of different work of equal—or equivalent—social value. Here we will continue to use the more neutral *equality.*

CHAPTER 7

1. This model was developed by Stewart Emery.
2. Robert Johnson, *We.* (San Francisco: Harper & Row, 1983), p. 52.
3. Psychoanalyst Alice Miller wrote a book entitled *For Your Own Good* (New York: Farrar, Strauss & Giroux, 1983), a cogent indictment of cruel and abusive child rearing practices and their dire consequences in adulthood.
4. The model was developed by Robert J. Sternberg of Yale University. See "The Three Faces of Love," by Robert J. Trotter, *Psychology Today,* September 1986, pp. 46–54.
5. William H. Masters, Virginia R. Johnson, and Robert C. Kolodny, *Human Sexuality,* second ed. (Boston: Little, Brown and Company, 1985), p. 399.
6. According to Masters, Johnson, and Kolodny, *Human Sexuality,* a *Cosmopolitan* survey completed in 1980 found that half of married women eighteen to thirty-four and 69.2 percent of married women thirty-five or older had had extramarital sex. But according to data collected by Blumstein and Schwartz in a survey conducted in 1983 with a large sample ($N = 3606$), only 21 percent of wives had any form of extramarital sex (p. 397).
7. Trotter, "The Three Faces of Love," p. 48.
8. *A Course in Miracles* (Tiburon, Calif.: Foundation for Inner Peace, 1976), p. 315.

CHAPTER 8

1. *The Passionate Life: Stages of Loving* (San Francisco: Harper & Row, 1983), p. 14.
2. For an extensive treatment of second-order change, refer to *Change: Principles of Problem Formation and Problem Resolution,* by Paul Watzlawish, Ph.D., John Weakland, Ch.E., and Richard Fisch, M.D. (New York: W. W. Norton, 1974).
3. Adapted from *Transformers: The Therapists of the Future,* by Jacquelyn Small, M.S.W. (Marina del Rey, Calif.: De Vorss & Company, 1982), p. 209.

4. In *Tao: The Watercourse Way,* by Allan Watts with the collaboration of Al Chuang-Liang Huang (New York: Pantheon Books, 1975), p. 76.

5. Adapted from the Promises of *Alcoholics Anonymous,* 3rd ed. (New York, Alcoholics Anonymous World Services, Inc., 1976), pp. 83–84.

Copyright Acknowledgments

from *Alcoholics Anonymous* adapted and reprinted with permission of Alcoholics Anonymous World Services, Inc. "T/A Script Inventory" adapted from one developed by Ralph L. Miller, Ph.D., and Dawn Miller, M.S. Used with permission of the authors. "Relationship History Form," by Sue Evans, L.P.